ACTIVE TALK

ACTIVE TALK

THE EFFECTIVE USE OF
DISCUSSION IN LEARNING

MORRY VAN MENTS

Kogan Page, London / St Martin's Press, New York

This book is dedicated to the memory of persecuted children, men and women whose voices were untimely silenced.

First published in 1990 in Great Britain by
Kogan Page Limited
120 Pentonville Road
London N1 9JN

British Library Cataloguing in Publication Data

A CIP record for this book is available from the British Library.

ISBN (UK) 07494 0246 6

First published in 1990 in the United States of America by St Martin's Press Inc., 175 Fifth Avenue, New York, NY 10010

Library of Congress Cataloging in Publication Data

A CIP catalog record for this book is available from the
Library of Congress

, Bucks
s plc

Contents

Preface   9

Chapter 1. Introduction   11

Why talk?   11
Writing versus speaking   13
Using discussion for teaching   16
Background   18
The structure of talk   20
Discussion and democracy   22

Chapter 2. Discussion   25

Introduction   25
Classification of structures   28
Advantages/disadvantages   31
Conducting a discussion   32
Role of the leader   43
Leaderless groups   46
The position in the curriculum   47
Uses   49
Problems and special techniques   52

Chapter 3. Debriefing   59

Introduction   59
The purpose of debriefing   61
The logic of debriefing   64
Techniques   69
Conclusion   73

Chapter 4. The art of questioning   **76**

   The uses of questioning   76
   Types of questions   77
   Sequence of questioning   79
   Problems and pitfalls   81

Chapter 5. Listening and the active student   **84**

   The need to listen   84
   The process of listening   85
   Understanding and interpretation   87
   Techniques   88
   Problems   90
   Environment   92
   'Groupthink'   93

Chapter 6. Argument and debate   **97**

   The use of argument   97
   Debating   99
   The process of argument   100
   Structure   100
   Evidence   101
   Logic and reasoning   103
   Meaning   105
   Methods of argument   108
   Fallacies   113
   Getting the floor   119

Chapter 7. Presentation and persuasion   **121**

   Origins of oratory and rhetoric   121
   Structure   122
   Persuasion   123
   The audience   126
   Style and technique   128
   Giving information   132
   Holding the audience   134

References and further reading   **139**

Index   **141**

In your relations with others, exercise imagination, understanding and sympathy. Listen patiently, and seek whatever truth other people's opinions may contain for you. Think it possible that you may be mistaken. In discussion, avoid hurtful and provocative language; do not allow the strength of your convictions to betray you into making statements or allegations that are unfair or untrue.

From *Advices and Queries* London Yearly Meeting of the Religious Society of Friends (1964)

Preface

Those who are concerned with the problems of teaching in a rapidly changing and stressful environment will know that the greatest overall change in education has been the move towards practical, active and dynamic learning. The more traditional methods of teaching used to be characterized by the term 'chalk and talk', but the word 'talk' in that phrase referred to the teacher talking, not the pupil. The idea of talking now applies equally to students, who are encouraged to interact with the teacher and their fellow students; there is now a greater emphasis on the use of speech rather than a dependency on the written word.

It is not that discussion is not accepted as a teaching method. Indeed the teacher can often be heard to say 'Let's discuss that' and in the course of that discussion the comments 'You didn't listen', 'It doesn't make sense', or 'You must learn to put over your point of view' may be heard. It is rather that more than just enthusiasm and encouragement are needed for the effective use of discussion. The teacher can make better use of classroom time if there is more structure to the session, and a deeper understanding of what is involved.

In order to enter the world of work and the community, and to progress through life, students must first of all be able to organize their experiences and learn from them. This is the central theme of the two chapters on the use of discussion and debriefing which follow the Introduction. The next thing that the student must tackle is the process of interacting as a member of a group or team; the following two chapters on questioning and listening cover some of the skills which assist this process. The emphasis of the book changes during this section, away from the teacher's role of leading and structuring towards the students' need for guidance on presenting themselves in discussion. The last two chapters on argument and persuasion therefore concentrate on showing the importance of being able to analyse fallacious arguments and put forward a case.

This book is designed as a guide to those who use discussion methods in their teaching. It also specifically deals with the subject of debriefing after using simulations and role-play activity. It is aimed mainly at teachers in schools and colleges, but industrial trainers, group facilitators and youth leaders will find it of equal value. It should be of practical use to those who are trying to develop new teaching methods in response to the demands of the National Curriculum in Britain, and the emphasis on personal skills in the United States.

The material is presented as a mixture of background information and practical checklists and suggestions. The Introduction discusses the use of the spoken word in the past and present, and the following chapter on discussion presents the core material of the book. Other chapters deal with specific subjects and can be read in any order. For classroom use it will be found that the chapters on listening, argument and persuasion can be used directly as teaching material while the chapter on debriefing provides the teacher with a logical sequence for making the most effective use of this procedure.

I would like to thank all of my friends and colleagues who have made the process of learning about the skills of discussion and debate a highly enjoyable one. My family are well used to the idea of argument and I am grateful to them for their forbearance over the years; in particular to my wife, Jennifer, whose perception and insight has consistently maintained my interest and pleasure in the joys of conversation.

Morry van Ments
September 1990

1. Introduction

Why talk?

The old idea of learning depended on the concept of the mind, or at least part of the mind, being a blank sheet waiting to receive knowledge. The job of the teacher was to provide a steady flow of information and wisdom to fill these spaces. The educated person would later be able to refer mentally to this encyclopedia of knowledge in order to deal with day-to-day problems. Even in adult life there were still empty spaces to be filled, and therefore the adult could continue to learn in the same way as the schoolchild. A large part of the process was devoted to repetition and rote learning because this was the way in which items could be retained in the memory.

Our understanding of the learning processes now paints a very different picture of the way in which the brain functions and of the interaction between the student and the teacher. Both general education and specific training depend on the development of a frame of reference, an outline picture of the world, in the mind of the student. All events of which we are aware are interpreted and remembered in relation to this model of the world which we carry in our heads. The development of this model is organic; it changes and grows by constant adjustment as a result of experience.

Students therefore learn by being brought into structured contact with the information, techniques and methods which they need. The environment in which this takes place must be one in which there is opportunity to select what is most appropriate, and to integrate it into the student's mental framework. This both helps the student to remember what has been learnt, and also modifies the framework to take the new knowledge into account.

In plain language, then, learning is an active process. Teachers are increasingly expected to involve students in active learning through exercises, projects, simulations and role-plays, and through visits from outside speakers and to outside venues such as factories and public services. It is not sufficient to provide these experiences for the students, however; there is a parallel need to ensure that the key points of the experience are selected for further thought before they are lost in the generality of impressions. Having selected points for consideration, they can be looked at in detail to clarify their meaning and future implications for further learning. The best way of achieving these goals is by a period of carefully structured debriefing and discussion in which students have the opportunity to select aspects of these experiences to integrate into their own view of the world.

The role of the teacher in this context is that of a facilitator who enables the learners to reflect critically on their experiences, encourages them to explore different perspectives and consider how their knowledge is rooted in personal and social circumstances, and acts as a guide towards sources of knowledge and information. Part of this process will consist of teaching students by and through a structured dialogue to construct knowledge from their own resources. The tutor may moreover use his or her own subject expertise to provide problems which challenge the students and strengthen their capacity to seek and apply the resources to deal with them in practice.

Discussion enables students to be critical in their selection of key points, to recapitulate the experience and rehearse it so as to implant it in short-term memory (which has limited capacity), and to formulate a new schema which will enable them to retain knowledge and information in the long term. But the use of discussion goes much further than this. It is becoming increasingly important for students to work as members of a group or team and to communicate easily and effectively with others; education which fails to equip students to deal with the realities of the world is seen as deficient. One of the commonest skills which is needed is that of taking an effective part in verbal discourse; in other words talking and discussing matters of concern. Students must be taught how to listen to what others are saying, to analyse their arguments, and compare them with their own experiences. They must be able to clarify their own thoughts, to present them to others in their group, and to defend them logically and persuasively when challenged. Talking is an essential part of this process. It enables students to assess the importance of what they have experienced, and gives them an opportunity to integrate new information into their scheme of things.

This book, then, follows this logic of student needs. The remainder of this introduction explores the differences between the spoken and written word and in particular points to the powerful and essential role of discussion in teaching.

Writing versus speaking

The advent of printing in the fifteenth century brought about a radical change in the way in which people communicated. It was easy to see the advantages of the written word; it enabled people to correct their thoughts before revealing them to others, to use reference books, to communicate with others at a remote time and place, and to keep a permanent record of what they wanted to say. Writing enables the reader to know the author's thoughts even though the author is not there; the reader can go at his or her own pace and jump forwards and backwards at will; he or she can read sections again or refer to other written material to elucidate meaning.

But there is a high price to pay for these advantages. The author cannot know the reader's purpose in reading a book, nor how much experience and skill that reader already has. Explanations and examples cannot be related to each reader's particular situation. In short, the written word, for all its virtues, is a one-way communication. The spoken word is a two-way communication, it offers the chance of correcting misunderstandings, using the expressive power of the voice, following up individual needs, establishing rapport and ensuring that the speaker conveys the full sense of what he or she wants to say, and that those who listen gain all the knowledge and information they need at that particular moment.

In recent years we have seen a revival in the use of the spoken word for mass communication. Many forms of modern communication rely on the spoken word: the telephone, radio, television. Even the computer, until now tied to the keyboard, is struggling to break free and use voice communication for giving and receiving instructions. The pre-printing age was the age of what Walter Ong (1982) calls primary oracy, where utterances followed a certain structure and were, as we shall see later, additive, redundant, agonistic, balanced and dialectic. The new oracy is known as secondary oracy and differs from the primary one in that it addresses an invisible audience, makes short presentations, is closely controlled, and has a definite finishing point.

There is also a parallel shift in the requirements for industrial training and in education. Increasingly employers are realizing that the key to the smooth running of industry lies in better interpersonal relations, greater individual responsibility and initiative, and on the collaborative working of small groups by negotiation. In the community there is a growing awareness among social workers of the importance of family relationships in providing a stable framework for young people. As families fragment and disperse, young people need to understand how to integrate into the community around them, to negotiate for their needs in a rational way, and to use discussion and debate rather than violence to achieve their ends. All of these developments rely on good communication and most of that communication will be in the context of talking in small groups.

As has already been noted, there is an increasing emphasis on the use of experiential learning methods in schools and colleges. All kinds of practical experiences are being presented to the student: field placements, projects, structured exercises, role-play, simulations, case studies, skill practice, action research, discovery learning, work experience. All demand a period of discussion and debriefing to ensure that the lessons have been learnt, and there is therefore a premium on the spoken word once more. Moreover teachers know that learning may encompass far more than just facts. It also includes acquiring an awareness of ideas, values, skills, and procedures, and these qualities cannot be expressed as well by the written word as by speech.

There is a long way to go in reviving the arts of speech. The modern generation distrust language's ability to express a true and accurate picture of reality. They rely on phrases such as 'you know', 'like', 'I mean' and 'sort of' to pad out their discourse. A statistical study of telephone speech revealed a vocabulary of only 737 words used in 96 per cent of conversations. People speak more but say less. It is perhaps time to look a little more towards speaking and less towards writing, which is filling our waste baskets with more and more paper.

It is unfortunate to say the least of it therefore that schools and colleges have concentrated on the skills of writing and reading, while in the world outside it is increasingly verbal skills that are in demand. No business enterprise can exist without good verbal communication with its workforce or customers, no service can operate efficiently without the empathy with its clients that can only be achieved by talking to each other. Industrial disputes, political persuasion, presenting one's case . . . all are part of everyday working life; they all make use of discourse and discussion.

The basic aims of education have undergone several changes in the past two or three decades. The current thinking is well expressed by the Education Reform Act passed by the British government in 1988. It states its aims as 'to promote the spiritual, moral, cultural, mental and physical development of pupils and society; and to prepare pupils for the opportunities, responsibilities and experiences of adult life.' The second part of this statement is vitally important because it sets the context for the legitimate interest of industry, of the world of employment, in the school and college curriculum. The world of work is a vital part of the 'experiences of adult life', and this world is set within an organizational structure in which the social environment makes it necessary to develop personal relationships in order to carry out the tasks which have to be done. This calls for the use of personal skills of communication quite apart from any particular subject or craft skills. These skills of verbal communication, once learnt, are transferrable to a wide range of situations.

At a time when everyone has to read large amounts of written material, or is bombarded by graphic images, it is important to stop and reconsider the power, potential and pleasures of the spoken word. Every day we are faced by voluminous newspapers, individualized mail-shots, lengthy word-processed documents and reports, faxed items which demand attention, and of course the latest efforts of the desktop publishing brigades. In an endeavour to escape this avalanche of paper we may turn to our computer, or TV screen. No respite there; we are targeted by dazzling displays of graphic art, by interactive and wordy computer programs, and increasingly by a combination of the two in the shape of interactive video.

Do these modes of communication really have such an advantage over the face-to-face discussion, argument, and reasoning which mankind used for centuries before the advent of writing? This book is an attempt to show how the oral tradition, the spoken word, the exchange of ideas as they actually occur, have qualities and potential which have been overlooked by the technocrats. It will also show the reader the most effective way to make use of the natural and instinctive verbal abilities which every human being has, in order to teach, guide and develop the student's potential.

In this day and age it may seem a little odd to be writing a book about talking. After all the invention of printing with moveable typeface in the mid-fifteenth century enabled those who could read to store and transmit their knowledge without the need to memorize and convey their thoughts by word-of-mouth. Now television, with its forerunners of photography and the cinema, has built on the power of the graphic image to change the whole way in which we receive information. The persuasive quality of the reasoned argument or the emotions roused by an eloquent speech have been replaced by the 30-second commercial or the single dramatic image brought into our living rooms. It is made evident daily that a picture is worth a thousand words; political ideas, soap powder, compassion for disaster victims, are all sold to us by the cunning graphics and dramatic pictures on our screens.

Not only has there been a revolution in the way in which information is brought to us, but the storage and retrieval of knowledge, once a laborious process of careful research and diligent copying, is now managed by computers and their accompanying file storage. It is no longer necessary to remember large quantities of information and ways of retrieving it. The computer will provide a multitude of pathways to the knowledge we require; it will suggest avenues of exploration and search on keywords through vast banks of data.

With all of these facilities at our disposal, why should it be important, indeed essential, to develop those skills which are best described as 'talking'? The answer is very simple. It is through those skills, and only through them, that it is possible to clarify our thinking and the thinking of others. The seminar, conversation, the committee meeting, debriefing and group discussion are all means of exposing ideas and thoughts to the analysis of other minds. They are the method by which we can confirm our understanding, crystallize our thoughts, and check the meanings and underlying emotions which are the currency of communication.

Using discussion for teaching

Discussion plays a central part in our lives. It is the means by which we organize our thoughts and make contact with the thinking of others; it is an activity which brings enjoyment, learning and decision-making together. Many writers, starting with Pericles in the fifth century BC, have pointed out that the worst thing is to rush into action before the consequences have been properly debated.

The discussion group appears in a variety of guises. Consider for example the group of citizens brought together in the village hall to consider a local plan for a by-pass round the village. Or an audience on television discussing some moral or political issue. Other examples might be a problem-solving session in the laboratory where a group of scientists are working, a literary seminar at the local college, or a self-help group meeting to discuss mutual problems. In business, half our time seems to be spent in meetings, negotiations and disputes, while even at home there are occasions when families may get together to discuss their affairs.

The dynamics of group interaction are such that in a typical group discussion a number of processes are going on at the same time. The group leader must of course be aware of the range of changes that are happening; any human interaction implies changes in emotional as well as intellectual attitudes. The focus of our attention in this book, however, is that of learning in the sense of the acquisition of knowledge and skills, and the other more personal and emotional aspects of oral communication will only be touched in passing.

The use of discussion as a technique for teaching centres on the fact that it is above all else a means of escaping from our own individual perceptions of the world, with all their circumscriptions and boundaries into which we would otherwise be locked. It adds to the richness of understanding and enables us to make contact with the minds of others in the most direct way possible. For the teacher or trainer it offers the opportunity to show the relevance of what is being taught to the individual student's concerns and experience. There are clearly some advantages to the printed word, not least its permanence and availability at any time. But printing forces a fixed precision and artificial spacial structure on to words (this was not always the case; the very earliest printed texts were laid out in the same form and emphasis as the words would be spoken). This graphical layout in neat blocks of text prevents the mind from moving in its natural way which is to manipulate the sounds of words. When we think, we tend to think in patterns of words, and these patterns tend to be evoked by the sound the word or phrase makes. Words are made of sounds, not letters. As Plato pointed out, 'Thought and speech are the same; only the former, which is a silent inner conversation of the soul with itself, has been given the special name of thought.' Most people have a much greater facility of expression with oral communication than with the written word and can use it to convey and receive a greater range and depth of emotion. Thoughts are framed in words; pictures only have meaning under special conditions, and even then they are often framed by words.

Oral communication has a number of advantages over written

communication in the field of teaching. It has an immediacy which cannot be matched, there is an earthiness and realism about it and it enables the teacher or trainer to use informal language and a lack of pretension which mirrors more closely the participants and catches people where they are. Immediate feedback ensures that the student can query those parts which were not understood and it helps the tutor to identify quickly the strong and weak points of the students. The written word has to be constructed to suit a wide variety of people who will be reading it in a range of circumstances. It therefore has to simplify and smooth out awkward aspects which cannot be explained without a great deal of trouble, unlike dialogue or discussion where anything can be injected in the knowledge that appropriate explanation can be given if necessary.

In terms of teaching, discussion offers the opportunity to question, clarify, explain and defend one's arguments. Although it is possible to record a great deal in writing, real experts can always improve on anything they have written if they are given the opportunity to meet the student face-to-face. It is not only the fact that dialogue, as the name suggests, is a two-way process and therefore offers the means of amending and clarifying what has been said; it is the fact that there is a subtlety which can be utilized in speaking because of the variations in expression that are possible. Speech, in other words, is responsive, flexible and accessible.

Background

It may come of something of a surprise to those who think of rhetoric and oratory in terms of someone hectoring, blustering and ranting to know that the study of these skills (of rhetoric and oratory that is) was part of the national curriculum of the Middle Ages. In those times the three basic arts were those connected with Logic, Mathematics and Rhetoric. There was good reason for this; after all it is essential to be able to handle quantities and numbers, and Logic and Rhetoric enabled one to communicate and persuade others of the righteousness of one's cause.

The process of teaching by the spoken word has been discussed by many authors in the educational field. Froebel, the founder of the kindergarten movement, argued for an approach to education in which the teacher shows both sides of the picture and encourages critical discussion. The ancient universities presented knowledge in lectures, arranging to examine the lecture in the seminar afterwards, a process which involved a certain amount of repetition to aid memorizing, and then debating the underlying meaning in a formal disputation. Although details have changed, this process of presentation, analysis, and synthesis is still at the heart of university education.

There is a misconception that language is basically what we read. This is not so. Language is so overwhelmingly oral by nature that of all the many thousands of languages spoken in the course of human history only around 106 have ever been committed to writing to a degree sufficient to produce literature. Of the 3,000 or so spoken languages that exist today only some 78 have a literature. Although writing enlarges the capacity for expression, by enlarging one's potential vocabulary with the aid of a dictionary for example, 'reading' text still means transforming it into an (unspoken) sound.

The essential difference between reading and writing, and speaking and listening lies in their relationship to time. Speaking is fluid, transient and ongoing. One cannot revise it, improve it, change or amend it as it flows along. The act of listening must coincide in time with the sounds of the speaker, whereas it is very rare for the reader to read at the same rate that the writer writes. This gives speech an immediacy and relevance which is bound to be missing in written material.

It is noticeable that the newspapers nowadays report very little of the speeches made by politicians and other notable people. A few years ago they printed whole speeches, then they settled for shorter versions; now they print very little verbatim, but only summarize what was said. The actual words seem to have lost their value. At the same time, however, television brings an ever increasing flood of talk into the home, and the telephone brings verbal interruptions in the office. Amid a maze of communication channels, there is an urgent need to understand and use the most natural and comfortable of them all – the conversation, or its more structured sibling, the discussion. In the course of learning to use conversation well, it is useful to bear in mind the three requisites of the well-spoken citizen as propounded by the Ancient Greeks, namely the ability to be logical and argue cogently, the ability to be persuasive and effective in the use of speech, and finally to mould one's discourse into an elegant, pleasing and harmonious whole: precepts which apply as much to today's world as they did before.

The structure of talk

Talk covers a wide range of activities. Those activities with which we are principally concerned in this book form a sub-group of speaking which has a purpose and a structure imposed on it. The essential quality of discussion is that it entails putting forward more than one point of view and it has a subject or subjects in view for consideration. The objective of a discussion may be to increase knowledge, but it can also be to improve understanding or critical judgment.

Verbal communication can be thought of as a mixture of four types:

Phatic

This is the name given to the lighthearted, social discourse of which O'Henry said it 'injects a few raisins into the tasteless dough of existence'. It is the stuff of everyday life and is an essential component of building relationships. Much of this speech is ritualistic, noticeably so on the telephone: 'How are you?', 'All the best', 'See you soon'. The mere exchange of words helps to bring people together. This type of intercourse has no agenda and no objective; it is enjoyable for its own sake.

Cathartic

This is a highly personal form of speech whose main purpose is to release emotional tension. Swearing is a simple example of this but there are less extreme examples in the areas of performance and counselling. One of the characteristics of this aspect of talking is that it is not normally recorded or referred to in detail afterwards.

Informative

As the name suggests, this has a specific purpose to share ideas and knowledge, to give out information, and to ensure understanding. It is the basis of educational talking, particularly in the more theoretical fields.

Persuasive

This is the practical face of talk. Talk as an instrument to change attitudes and produce decisions and actions.

Human communication consists of a procedure by which the original thought or concept in the mind of the speaker is coded into sounds and words, transmitted over a more or less noisy channel, and then decoded at the other end to form the image which is received by the listener. In such a complex process it is easy for misunderstandings to occur, but the strength of using discussion is that there is constant feedback on whether the listener has understood. There is a great danger that without this facility misunderstandings can occur, incomplete information can be allowed to influence us, and illogical arguments hold sway.

One of the most puzzling things about language is the way in which it manages to be at one and the same time so simple and yet so complex. After only a few years of life, normal children possess the entire linguistic system that allows them to utter and understand sentences they have not previously heard. The complexity of this skill is so great that it takes psycholinguists pages to analyse even a simple sentence. And yet the child finds it easier to speak than to read, do arithmetic, or swim. Speech behaviour is perhaps best regarded as an interaction, a game in which both speakers and listeners unconsciously know the rules of their speech communities and the strategies they may employ. Even such a simple act as addressing a stranger reveals a code for such things as age (sonny, youngster, old boy), status (John, sir, dear, sister), and profession (Doctor, Father, Your Worship).

This complexity is well typified by an acronym devised by Dell Hymes, quoted in Farb (1974), SPEAKING, which stands for the various components of the act of speaking, namely:

SETTING. The scene, the environment and atmosphere.
PARTICIPANTS. Who is part of the discussion and who is outside it, a culturally determined factor.
ENDS. The purpose of the discourse.
ACT SEQUENCE. The degree of structure or informality present.
KEY. The intonation or manner; serious, ironic, sarcastic.
INSTRUMENTALITIES. The actual dialect or language used.
NORMS. The accepted ways of behaving. Use of interruptions, silence, repetition, pauses, 'er's and 'um's.
GENRES. Types of speech, similar to the classification given above; greetings, farewells, questions, prayers, jokes, speeches.

The complexity of speech is what makes it human. The number of sound units (phonemes) in human speech can be easily assessed. It varies for different languages; for English there are about 45 phonemes, for Italian about 27, and for Hawaiian 13, for example. Animals can produce a similar number of different sounds; the chicken can produce 25 different sounds, the chimpanzee 25, the dolphin 28, and the fox 36. The major difference is that animals cannot combine these sounds in different ways to produce the almost infinite range of expressions which can convey all human thoughts. It is the complexity of these combinations that gives human languages their richness.

One of the reasons why tutors and teachers are resistant to using discussion methods is because they themselves were not taught by these methods. Not only does this inhibit their using the techniques, but, more important perhaps, they have little idea of the correct methods to use in order to get the best out of a session. Because speech appears to come so naturally to us, it is not always realized that it is possible to improve one's presentation. It is notable that both Abraham Lincoln and Winston Churchill were distinctly poor speakers in their youth.

As with many other things, the use of discussion as a technique is not difficult but without some thought it is all too easy to use it badly or ineffectively. Oral communication refers to the process of having something to say and saying it well so that those with whom the speaker is interacting are interested in maintaining the dialogue or discussion. It includes fluency, tone, the use of gestures, eye contact and facial expression, having the range of vocabulary and the capacity to relate contributions to the needs of the listeners. By following simple rules and guidelines it is possible to avoid common mistakes. In the end it is feasible to have at one's command possibly the most powerful tool in the teacher's resources.

The spoken word is the means by which we carry on most of our day-to-day communication even in this age of the computer. It is also the way in which we put our ideas across to others, try to change their attitudes and crystallize our thought and the consensus of views between ourselves and others when we have to make decisions. This book therefore covers a range of uses of speech in the worlds of education and work. For convenience it is arranged in chapters, but the practice of talking to others is so fundamental that there is considerable overlap between the ideas, concepts and precepts dealt with in the different chapters.

Discussion and democracy

The process of discussion is a powerful technique for teaching. At the same time there are certain aspects of it which support the democratic ideal and provide a platform for the exercise of equality. The basis of this proposition is that effective discussion assumes a willingness on the part of each participant to listen to others, to make an effort to understand their arguments and point of view, and to change one's own attitude if so persuaded. People do not start off with blank minds; the course of education is as much to do with changing behaviour and modifying understanding as it is about instilling new knowledge.

Discussion is a key element of the democratic process, a process which is increasingly being recognized as not only morally good but also an effective means for working groups to arrange their affairs. To operate well it is necessary for the participants to understand how to make the best use of discussion and to use it as a tool for exploring their needs and the solutions to their problems. One of the first things to learn is that it is only a genuine discussion if participants are willing to modify their opinions; otherwise it is an abstract debate. Even in negotiations the negotiators must be willing to change ground, otherwise they would reach an impasse.

The essence of democracy in action is that everyone has a respect for the opinions of others. It is impossible to conceive of a society which claimed to be democratic in which this cardinal rule was broken. It is also the foundation of discussion and runs as a thread through the rest of this book.

One word of warning is perhaps necessary before turning to the chapters which follow. There is a myth that running a discussion group requires less preparation than giving a straight lecture; this is far from the truth. In fact, unlike the normal lecturer, the tutor who leads a group in discussion requires to know the subject not merely in a linear way, but must literally know it backwards, forwards, sideways and round about, because there is no guarantee that the discussion will follow a logical, linear, or even continuous path. When one is dealing with multiple interlocking strands it is easy to get lost if one is not completely *au fait* with the subject. The effective discussion leader must be able to foresee the pattern of development and guide the members appropriately. The preparation needed is therefore more, not less, exacting than that for the average lecture.

The teacher or trainer who hopes to work effectively with discussion groups must acquire the ability to attend to detail while keeping an eye on and comprehending the overall view. He or she must appreciate different viewpoints and be receptive to new ideas. There should be tolerance and respect for problem students – or students with problems!

The task of those who want to use active discussion methods is not, therefore, an easy one. On the other hand the best teachers are those who continue to learn throughout their lives. Luckily, discussion is such an ubiquitous part of everyday life that there is no shortage of study material on which to work. It is both easy and interesting to observe the way in which people interact, argue, support each other, and generally go about their business. It is the most natural thing in the world to want to discuss something; it is one of the most fascinating things in the world to observe the complexity of interactions this produces. Those who want to improve their understanding of the processes involved will not run short of material for study.

2. Discussion

Introduction

Discussion must be one of the most widely used processes in education but is at the same time one of the most difficult of teaching techniques to use effectively. All too often the cry 'Let's discuss that' is a signal for rambling, aimless chat which fills time, but achieves very little. Because conversation is such a natural part of everyday life, it is assumed that a discussion will automatically structure itself to fulfil the unspoken objectives of the tutor. Discussion is not the same as conversation, however; it needs careful attention to both preparation and structure.

Discussion may be regarded as a process whereby two or more people exchange information or ideas in a face-to-face situation to achieve a goal. Note the importance of the face-to-face qualification; other forms of information exchange are less comprehensive and immediate than discussion.

The fact that people are talking freely to each other does not in itself mean that they are having a discussion. Talk which is socially generated is just conversation or chitchat; with some teachers this is the type and style of their so-called discussions. The characteristics of such situations are muddle, lack of continuity, and a sense of frustration among those who are trying to achieve something. In order to turn it into a discussion certain criteria must be fulfilled. The most obvious of these is that there should be a subject or subjects for discussion. This is not to say that the subject need be a narrow one, or closely defined. Indeed it may well be that the subject changes in the course of discussion. Nevertheless at any one time the participants should have a subject area clearly in their minds as a target to aim for; there must, in other words, be an intention to develop knowledge, understanding or judgment in some specific area.

There must normally be more than one point of view and those taking part in the discussion must initially be responsive to all of the points of view put forward. In practice there will also be a presupposition about the type of moral climate in which the discussion takes place. There is an implicit assumption that group members will be frank and open with each other, and not be devious or deliberately misleading. Because of this, people engaged in discussion make subconscious use of various devices in order to reduce the risk of self-exposure to participants. These are discussed in detail in the section on Problems and Special Techniques.

Another difference between conversation and discussion is the attitude to evidence, the way in which we react to other people's statements. In normal society, on social occasions, conversation is conducted on the assumption that people accept things at face value – on trust. Discussion relies on academic questioning of evidence, criteria, etc; it is essentially a formal rather than an informal activity. The participants must be disposed to examine the evidence in a critical and analytical way.

On the other hand, debriefing is also a structured process. The difference between discussion and debriefing, however, is that debriefing supposes that an activity has been undertaken which at least in some cases has been prepared or briefed beforehand. This activity may have led to a number of unresolved issues and misunderstandings which need to be cleared up, together with interpretations of actions within the event and learning points associated with the activity. Debriefing is a structured way of dealing with these outstanding points.

The reason that discussion is so often used as a part of the teaching curriculum is probably an unconscious recognition of the special qualities of speech in teaching students to think for themselves; discussion in a group allows students to test their conceptual ideas against one another and against reality just in the same way as testing on real objects confirms physical concepts. You may think that heating a piece of plastic will soften it, a practical test confirms or contradicts this idea and shows the differences, hitherto perhaps unsuspected, between types of plastic. Similarly you may think that the arguments against or for nuclear power are self-evident until you have to pursue the complexities of the case with others. Above all, however, there is no other way of teaching that is as popular with the students themselves.

It is possible in special situations to have a discussion in written textual form, but this is not as effective as oral discussion because the spoken word:

1. Produces quicker responses from the listener and hence is self-sustaining;
2. Is flexible – can be interrupted for clarification or to identify errors;
3. Has effects that can be monitored – one can gauge the response of listeners and adjust the level, speed and style of communication accordingly;
4. Is subtle – aided by non-verbal cues;
5. Tends more towards frankness; this is partly because of the use of less formal language and partly because the speed of interaction leaves no time for dissimulation and caution. There is also no feeling that everything is being put on permanent record;
6. Is accessible to all, including the illiterate.

Discussion is an interactive approach which recognizes individual differences and exploits them, it encourages students to discover their own strengths and weaknesses. It is also an environment in which divergence of views can, and should, be encouraged. This is in contrast to committees, where the objective is usually to arrive at a consensus view or at least at a decision which reflects a majority view. A committee is best steered on a convergent course towards a final point; a discussion group can be taken into wider and wider territory, ensuring that all aspects of the question are considered and that leads are followed up wherever possible. Leaders should not be afraid of an inconclusive ending; the aim is to get minds working, not to close them. Discussion is almost the only remaining vehicle nowadays for ensuring and protecting a divergence of views.

The importance of discussion as a means of acquiring knowledge is that it enables us to escape from our own individual perceptions with their circumscriptions and boundaries into which we would otherwise be locked. It adds to the richness and breadth of our understanding.

In our culture conversation consists of one person speaking at a time with no silences between; pauses and silences tend to get filled in by speech and this can lead to 'small talk', social clichés, and conventional wit and repartee. It is therefore necessary to change the procedure deliberately in order to convert a conversation into a discussion or debriefing. These changes in approach and style are at the root of the techniques for conducting an effective session.

Classification of structures

The major objective of discussion methods is usually to develop the students' ability to think, but we can distinguish a number of strands within this wide general aim. To begin with, it is useful to see that there are two basic types:

1. Reflective discussion – seeks an *understanding* of, among other things, the standards and criteria needed in order to make judgments;
2. Argumentative discussion – presupposes some *consensus* on the procedures whereby judgments can be verified or refuted and concentrates on how these criteria may apply in specific cases.

Since discussion is a special type of conversation, one way of classifying it is by means of the types of rules and conventions which mark out the discussion from idle chatter.

Intellectual – logical – cognitive

In a proper discussion participants must be prepared to give reasons for their beliefs and attitudes. They must be encouraged to explore the evidence on which beliefs are based rather than just saying, 'I think that chair looks awful', or 'Everyone knows it's unethical to accept gifts from salespeople', or 'Modern photographic papers don't give as good an effect as the old ones did'. Discussion can be stilted if people make a series of assertive statements with little to back them up; this will often lead to a series of unproductive silences. It is important therefore to teach students to proceed from their starting points with logical arguments and to give statements credence depending on their relevance and logical basis.

Procedural

A discussion should have some structure; this may be in the form of a written, or unwritten, agenda, or a set of objectives. There needs to be an accepted method of controlling the 'traffic' of talk, of deciding who should be holding the floor at any one moment. There should be an overt sequence of stages, ending with moves that bring the discussion to a close.

Social

The style of language used in a discussion is usually slightly more formal and explicit than that used in conversation. One aspect of the degree of formality is the extent to which students cite authorities for statements which they make, ie the source of their opinions or information. Likewise the sharpness, depth and detail of criticism will be greater. The amount of personal revelation is likely to be less than in an informal conversation with a friend, although this may depend upon the exact purpose of the discussion and the environment in which it is taking place. In most forms of discussion there is a progressive disclosure of attitudes and personal information as the participants develop confidence in one another.

There are various ways of classifying types of discussion. The following system derives from Harnack et al (1977):

Purposes

Personal: Social/Cathartic/Therapeutic/Learning/Self development;

Task: Decision making/Action/Appraisal (evaluative, investigative)/ Advisory (on policy)/Advisory (creation of new ideas, synthesis of ideas).

Circumstances

A spectrum of circumstances ranging from casual encounters, through voluntary but planned occasions, to organized situations planned by external bodies.

Form

There are many forms which classroom discussion can take. This list is derived from classifications suggested by various authors, including Bligh (1986) and Jaques (1984).

1. Debate. This is the typical form of public discussion.
2. Panel – with silent audience, audience participation, or with representatives of the audience questioning.
3. Forum/symposium – everyone takes part.
4. Buzz group – students are asked to work with their neighbour(s).
5. Peer tutoring – a type of buzz group in which there is a formal

acknowledgment of the way in which each student can listen to, and help the other one.

6. Snowball/pyramid – students work in pairs, then fours, then eights and so on.
7. Breaking a seminar into smaller groups – a good way of developing powers of analysis and argument.
8. Free discussion.
9. Controlled discussion.
10. Step-by-step – a particular form of controlled discussion in which a pre-programmed series of questions is used to draw out the students.
11. Cross-over – this is a good way of avoiding the need for a plenary. Participants are split into groups so that the number of participants roughly equals the number of groups (hence this is known as the 'square-root' system). Groups are lettered A, B, C . . . and participants numbered 1, 2, 3 . . . for each group.

The cross-over can then be organized as:

(a) One complete change. Groups A–F become groups 1–6. This produces a complete re-mix in one go, since all the number 1s go to group 1, all the 2s to group 2 etc.

(b) For each round, one person moves, eg clockwise between groups. First the number 1s move one group along then the number 2s move two groups along, then the 3s move three places and so on. This enables a mix and interchange of information and views without the need for a plenary.

Other ways of classifying discussions are:

Styles of approach

- Encounter
- Role-playing/games and simulations
- Brainstorm
- Synectics
- Associative
- Sensitivity, T-group, encounter group.

Formal frameworks

- Committee
- Conference

- Seminar
- Case studies – one particular example of the problem-centred approach
- Syndicates – another example of the problem-centred approach. The projects may be open ended, with the students choosing the topics
- Tutorials – to solve problems of the individual student
- Decision making
- Negotiating
- Debriefing
- Debating.

Discussion can be regarded as having two dimensions; the 'degree of structure' component versus the 'tutor dominated/student dominated' component.

Advantages/disadvantages

Some of the advantages and disadvantages of using discussion as a teaching technique are listed below.

Advantages

1. Participants become committed to carrying out actions that have been discussed.
2. It encourages the flexibility to modify opinions.
3. It is one of the most effective ways to change attitudes.
4. It recognizes individual differences and exploits them.
5. Discussion encourages students to discover their own strengths and weaknesses.
6. Opinions are exposed to others for comment and assumptions are uncovered.
7. Students can compare their personal beliefs and behaviour against public criteria and standards.
8. There is a cross-fertilization of ideas.
9. Practical experience is the most effective way to learn how to communicate as professionals in a particular subject. Students can acquire the language, conventions, and shared conceptual framework of their profession together with the necessary oral skills.

31

10. Discussion gives practical experience of team working.
11. It gives practice in the application of principles to problems.
12. There is an encouragement to use critical standards and a questioning attitude to evidence.
13. It encourages clear analytical thinking while at the same time allowing for explanation and clarification.
14. It is a powerful way of developing the individual both in self-regard and in social skills.
15. It satisfies social needs and is usually highly motivational for student and tutor.

Finally, two heads are better than one. There is a pooling of knowledge and experience. If one takes the analogy of a jigsaw, it should be possible to attach additional bits of information without rejecting earlier ones. Different pieces add up to a single picture, not alternative views. Aristotle said that, 'Those feasts to which many contribute may excel those provided at one man's expense'

Disadvantages/Limitations

1. Discussion takes time.
2. It requires special skills from the leader.
3. There is a dilution of personal responsibility.
4. One cannot use it in an emergency (for decision making).

Conducting a discussion

1. The framework

In conducting a discussion, one can argue either for a logical step-by-step development or for just throwing ideas at random into the pool and allowing members of the group to abstract what is of particular interest to them and make their own connections. But the question of the efficiency of the process must be considered, especially if time is short, as it often is. There is an inherent contradiction about the conduct of productive discussion: on the one hand there is a wish to promote a free-flowing interchange of ideas and views, on the other there is an awareness that some form of structure, as in a committee, is more likely to make efficient use of the time. The answer is to use a series of guidelines or principles to help structure the process.

In order to make the best use of a period of discussion one needs to impose a framework. There must be an intention to develop knowledge, understanding or judgment, and the intentions and structure must be understood and agreed by the participants; a type of 'contract' must be made. The advantage of agreeing a joint undertaking is that it enables one to make the authority relationships more explicit and formal. This helps to avoid an unconscious sliding into conventional authority relationships. Effective learning is facilitated by formal (not necessarily conventional) structures and procedures. It should be realized that rules and structures are devices which protect and reassure the timid and less self-assured.

There is also, of course, a powerful argument against too much structure and for a more diffuse, inconsequential discussion. The comparison is with the activity of browsing in a library or bookshop; there is greater serendipity, greater participation. The balance for any particular discussion is a matter for the leader to decide.

Students tend to be afraid of revealing their own weaknesses, they prefer boredom rather than revealing the extent of their incompetence. They therefore have to be encouraged to be open. If students are to be encouraged to expose their ideas, attitudes, and beliefs to public discussion and analytical criticism, then an atmosphere must be created where participants have a high self-esteem, self-assurance and the confidence and honesty to allow their opinions to be challenged and changed. But this is itself one of the functions performed by the act of discussion. It is necessary, then, to use some of the initial discussion periods, or the initial part of the single discussion in order to develop this atmosphere. The leader must also be careful to maintain it throughout the whole session or series of sessions.

The basic rule is to start with small groups, short periods and simple tasks. Development is achieved by increasing the size of group, length of period and difficulty of task.

2. *Choosing the group and its structure*

The composition of the group must be related to the main purpose for which the discussion is being held. Normally there will be a mixture of objectives but they can be grouped under three headings: to learn and acquire knowledge, to allow students an opportunity to practise their powers of expression, and to create something or make decisions.

Where the emphasis is on learning, students at the same level should be grouped together. They learn from each other and the quicker ones will explain to the slower. Where the emphasis is on expression, introverts and extroverts are best allocated their own separate groups. Otherwise there is a danger that the extroverts will swamp the introverts. Where the emphasis is on creativity or decision making, it is best to use mixed groups; these provide a range of experience and knowledge, and the tensions will stimulate the participants.

The size of a group is an important factor in determining its effectiveness. Large groups (up to thirty or so) can solve specific technical problems since they are more likely to have access to specific information. A seminar group (or workshop as it is sometimes known) where a leader is taking the group through a process of learning, is best conducted with between ten and twenty participants. Small groups (eight or fewer) reach consensus on opinions more rapidly, while personal teaching in tutorials is best done with fewer than six students.

The time at which the session is held must be chosen with due regard to the preparation needed and to other activities which may need to relate to the discussion period. Often, of course, it is impossible to choose the particular moment because of other constraints, but it should be borne in mind whenever possible. More important however is the need to allow a sufficient length of time. This is almost always overlooked in practice because the discussion period comes last and the other activities overrun. If discussion is to be used seriously then sufficient time has to be given to it; this may mean deliberately curtailing other activities if they are likely to overrun.

3. Preparing the environment

It is not always possible to choose the size and shape of the room. Where there is a choice the room should be square rather than oblong, with sufficient space to move behind chairs but not so large as to intimidate the participants. The type of chair must strike a balance between comfort and formality. In general it is wise to avoid completely informal arrangements such as easy chairs or students sitting on the floor. If they are too informal it encourages the idea that a conversation is to take place rather than a discussion. The best arrangements are upright seats in a circle, arc or square. It is an advantage to have tables, provided that they are not too large; they give the student a feeling of security and a place for papers. Moreover, it is more difficult to withdraw from the discussion by moving one's chair back when there are tables as well. If the layout is in an arc, for the group to have a presentation or video for example, it is better for the tutor to sit at one end. Otherwise the tutor acts as a barrier between students, or as a focal point in the middle.

In considering the layout of the seating, the principle to follow is that distances must be small enough to maintain eye-contact; this leads to a number of different layouts such as the circle, horseshoe, semi-circle or rectangle. These shapes give different emphases on the role of the leader; they also occupy varying amounts of space in the room. Note that, as with committees, the position opposite the leader is the position of greatest power and control.

One particular layout is the multiple-horseshoe shape (see Figure 2.1). Note the use of a chair placed at the open end for the tutor to circulate. The length of each side should be no greater than three people because you can lean past one person to speak, but not two.

When considering the room layout it is worth remembering that students should have easy access to the blackboard, flip-chart etc,

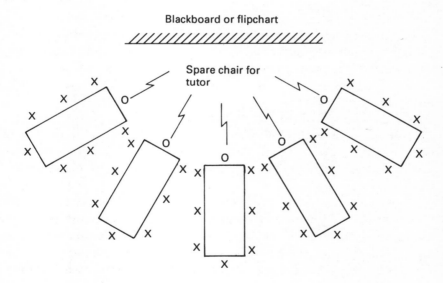

Figure 2.1 *Multiple horseshoe layout*

otherwise they will be discouraged from taking a fully participatory role.

Although the layout of furniture is important, like most things the rearrangement of seating to get the perfect result can itself create considerable disturbance to a relaxed atmosphere. It is best to keep a balance between the ideal layout and unnecessary fuss in rearrangement. There is also the question of the 'ownership' of the room, both in the physical sense of having access to a room where if necessary the discussion can overrun, and also in the psychological sense of a room in which the participants can feel some sense of ownership – in other words a freedom to relax and speak their minds without a feeling of being on someone else's territory. Of course in practice they are bound to be meeting in a room which technically belongs to someone else; nevertheless it is possible to convey an atmosphere which belongs more closely to the participants than to an impersonal room, or a room which is set out for another purpose. For this reason it is useful to involve students in arranging the room, quite apart from the advantage of having more helping hands.

4. Beginning the session

At the start of a session, there should be an expectation of belonging and enjoyment, sharing of ideas and experience. The tutor must ensure that everyone feels at ease, that there is a sense of orderliness and adequacy. Part of this process is the setting of 'ground rules' or a 'contract'. These terms are used variously to mean the conventions by which the discussion will be run or the extent to which the participants are expected to take responsibility for the degree of self-revelation which they exercise. At all events it is important to reach a mutual understanding with the participants on how the session is to be conducted.

Conventions should be made clear, for example whether or not to speak through the Chair. If notes should be taken then it is worth emphasizing the need to take notes of other students' contributions as well as of those of the tutor. It should be made clear who will be responsible for introducing which subject and the tutor should emphasize the importance of not being afraid to admit ignorance or uncertainty.

A good strategy at the start is to make an opportunity deliberately for everyone to say something early on so as to allay fears of speaking out aloud for the first time.

One preparatory move in starting a discussion is to ensure that the whole group agrees the need to generate a quality of discussion which is objective and open. If this is not generally understood, any intervention by the tutor will be seen as imposing authority instead of helping to make the discussion as effective as possible.

Before starting the discussion proper, the tutor should try to make the students feel an integral part of the process. He or she should clarify the purpose of the session, for example to:

- Pool knowledge;
- Explore different perspectives, particularly in controversial issues;
- Create empathy;
- Help self-development;
- Stimulate conjecture, creativity;
- Practise refutation and the use of dialectic processes.

In particular the teacher should be sure to clarify whether there is to be an element of assessment going on or not.

The tutor should identify the topic and its components, and give clear objectives and rational aims. Often it is useful to spell out the issues involved. The tutor may find it helpful to use hand-outs or audio-visual aids such as a film or video to set the scene. If the group is set tasks to do then these must be set at an appropriate level; one technique for setting tasks is to ask specific questions with an indication of the depth of answer required.

5. Ways of starting

Starting the actual discussion is a question of choosing from a variety of methods according to the taste and style of the tutor and the type of group and subject matter. Although discussions often start with the teacher asking, 'Who would like to start?', this can easily lead to the most articulate student dominating the group, or the discussion setting off on an ill-chosen and misleading path. It is more effective to give the group an initial framework to get them started. The following list is intended to give some ideas of the range of possibilities.

1. Buzz groups. Split the group into smaller units and give them

something general to discuss such as the value of the subject/text to the course.

2. Ask for one concrete image related to the subject from each student. It is often easier to focus on a concrete image than to talk about the subject in the abstract. The concrete image may be literally a picture, or it may be a description of a situation or event.
3. Ask each student to produce, say, six statements 'worth making'. That is to say they are clear, succinct, and sufficiently controversial to require careful thought. Not platitudes, trivialities, vague abstractions, assertions no one is likely to dispute or which would make no difference in practice. Statements must be limited to one sentence.
4. Break into smaller groups and give them a task such as finding a relevant quotation. Students may be asked to find one from a library of books in the room. This will get them moving and possibly exchanging ideas. Allow 15–20 minutes for this.
5. Place students physically on either side and ask them to debate a subject. Neutrals can move from one side to the other during discussion.
6. Set up a simple role-play. This can be done in pairs or trios.
7. Set the scene with audio-visual aids.
8. In a more formal way, the tutor can start with a short prepared statement summarizing the point reached last time, giving alternative possibilities to discuss, and indicating the lines of discussion expected.

It is worth noting that the discussion can be started by a group member or visitor; it does not have to be the official tutor who starts.

6. Guiding the discussion

During the course of the discussion the tutor must ensure that all the information needed is readily to hand, give out materials and ensure an adequate supply of texts and notes. The discourse must be kept on track, and diversions into the highways and byways reasonably limited; where appropriate, evidence should be looked for or provided.

In order to clarify ambiguous, vague, or irrelevant statements, the tutor should ask questions and request the speakers to show how their contributions connect with those of others and what their relevance is.

One of the key functions of the discussion leader is to interpret the contributions within a logical framework and to indicate the corollaries and consequences. This also gives the opportunity to point out the logic of what is said, or the lack of it. This is a suitable point at which to show how to distinguish between ideas and people, between the message and the messenger, and consequently how ideas may be challenged without appearing to threaten people.

Throughout the session, the tutor must keep in mind the need to stimulate, motivate, and maintain a group spirit. A diversity of views should be welcomed. At the same time the tutor must keep an eye on the time and help the group to complete its business within the allotted timespan.

Another way to guide the discussion is by adhering to a sequence of activities such as the 'Group Cognitive Map' proposed by Hill (1969). These particular activities are specifically intended for the discussion of a prior reading assignment but they provide a useful framework for other types of discussion. The sequence is as follows:

1. Define terms;
2. Make a general statement of the message;
3. Identify the main themes;
4. Allocate time (exclude items already understood);
5. Discuss the themes – try to understand the author's meaning;
6. Integrate new knowledge with other knowledge;
7. Discuss the application of material;
8. Evaluate individual presentation (personal observations);
9. Evaluate group performance.

It is tempting to think that a vigorous discussion is necessarily a good one. In many cases of course this is true, but it is as well to bear in mind that it is quality which should be encouraged rather than quantity (unless it is specifically a creativity session). Silence can be valuable in providing thinking time. The same can be said for the pace of the discussion. This relates both to the speed with which individual contributions are delivered and also to the rate at which they follow one another. A relatively slow pace is the ideal to aim for. This is easier to achieve in a large mixed group where there will be multiple levels of discussion going on and the more able students are less likely to get bored. All members gain from a variety and succession of points of view. The slower ones gain from a freedom to ask when they do not understand.

Throughout the discussion, the tutor should be aware of the signals

Proposing   Behaviour which puts forward a new concept, suggestion or course of action (and is actionable).

Building   Behaviour which extends or develops a proposal which has been made by another person (and is actionable).

Supporting   Behaviour which involves a conscious and direct declaration of support or agreement with another person or his concepts.

Disagreeing   Behaviour which involves a conscious, direct and reasoned declaration or difference of opinion, or criticism of another person's concepts.

Defending/attacking   Behaviour which attacks another person or defensively strengthens an individual's own position. Defending/attacking behaviours usually involve overt value judgements and often contain emotional overtones.

Blocking/difficulty stating   Behaviour which places a difficulty or block in the path of a proposal or concept without offering any alternative proposal and without offering a reasoned statement of disagreement. Blocking/difficulty stating behaviour therefore tends to be rather bald, eg 'It won't work,' or 'We couldn't possibly accept that.'

Open   Behaviour which exposes the individual to risk of ridicule or loss of status. This behaviour may be considered as the opposite of defending/attacking, including within this category admissions of mistakes or inadequacies, provided that these are made in a non-defensive manner.

Testing understanding   Behaviour which seeks to establish whether or not an earlier contribution has been understood.

Summarizing   Behaviour which summarizes, or otherwise restates in a compact form, the content of previous discussions or considerations.

Seeking information   Behaviour which seeks facts, opinions or clarification from another individual or individuals.

Giving information   Behaviour which offers facts, opinions or clarification to other individuals.

Shutting out   Behaviour which excludes, or attempts to exclude, another group member (eg interrupting, talking over).

Bringing in   Behaviour which is a direct and positive attempt to involve another group member.

Table 2.1 *Behavioural categories*

Table reproduced from Rackham, N and Morgan, T (1977) *Behaviour Analysis in Training* McGraw Hill (UK) Ltd.

that are being given, the interactions that are taking place, and the roles which are played by different members of the group. Group dynamics is a subject all on its own and there are many books written about it, but Table 2.1 gives an outline of the sort of behavioural pattern to be expected.

7. *Rules of conversation*

The study of who speaks to whom, when, how, and to what end is referred to by Wardhaugh (1985) as the 'ethnography of speaking'. The control of the flow of speech in a discussion is in the hands of the participants except in very formal debating-type meetings. In normal life most people have acquired the ability to sense an opening in the conversation when they may start to speak; there are a variety of means by which people signal their need to come into the conversation, or the fact that they are coming to the end of their contribution. In some cases however students are less practised in the art of getting in on a conversation; everyone therefore needs to be aware of their responsibility for seeing that the less assertive members of the group have a chance to contribute.

Just as the leader or tutor should follow a set of precepts in conducting the group, so the individual should have a set of guidelines to follow. A hand-out containing a list similar to that given below can with benefit be given to students as a model set of rules to follow.

- Do not argue about purely personal opinions or tastes.
- Stick to the issues. Be relevant.
- Do not listen only to yourself.
- Check out preconceptions and assumptions.
- Do not treat a question just as a signal to speak.
- Make an effort to understand; ask supplementaries.
- Make the wording of questions clear.
- Use each response as the basis for further questions or comment.
- Avoid appeals to authority and arguing *ad hominem* (about the person not the subject). Bad people are not always wrong.
- Beware of voting unless a decision is needed.
- Beware of using examples to prove rather than illustrate, but ask for examples to clarify understanding if necessary.
- Avoid anger, sarcasm, belittling, fastening on trivial mistakes.

These guidelines can equally, of course, be used by the tutor as a check on his or her own behaviour!

It is useful to be aware of the typical sequence in the development of a group. According to Tuckman, quoted in Bligh (1986), the temporal sequence in a small group is:

Form – setting ground rules, obtaining commitment;
Storm – conflict occurs, and argument;
Norm – there is an approach to consensus and summarizing;
Perform – the group gains insights, produces generalizations.

The leader should also be familiar with the basics of group dynamics. There are many textbooks on the subject, a typical practical one is that by David Jaques (1984) in which the following list of functions performed by group members is given:

- Initiating;
- Giving and asking for information;
- Giving and asking for reactions;
- Restating and giving examples;
- Confronting and reality-testing;
- Clarifying, synthesizing, summarizing;
- Timekeeping, keeping to the plan;
- Encouraging participation by others.

Similar lists will be found in other books.

The style or structure of a discussion period need not be fixed throughout the session. They can be alternated between free, informal sessions with spontaneity and freedom, and disciplined, urgent, structured sessions to take up the points which were made in the first sessions and pursue them logically.

8. Conclusion

The tutor should consider what has been covered, and how it can be used for the next step in the curriculum. The students should consolidate by reading around the subjects. Provision should be made for a permanent record. This written record may be arrived at by summarizing and asking the students to make notes, by having a 'reporter' prepare notes for the group, or by asking students to make their own notes as soon as possible afterwards.

Provision should be made for some feedback and evaluation of the session. Because the discussion will not always have followed a logical structure it may be difficult to evaluate in a linear way. One way of making an assessment is to look at the session as a 'balance sheet' of net gains and losses into which can be built a variety of elements such as criticisms, obligations, compliments, suggestions, changed relationships, new knowledge or new motivation.

Although it is natural for the leader to guide the discussion to a neat conclusion, not everyone agrees that this is necessarily a good thing. It has been argued that this is 'phoney', that it militates against a truly open discussion, and it has been called 'pseudo discussion'. It can turn into a situation where instead of the students being encouraged to think for themselves and follow the logic of their own arguments, they are really engaged in an investigation of the teacher's thought processes, and are reading clues in what becomes a series of disconnected endeavours to read the teacher's mind.

Role of the leader

The leader of a discussion group may take on different roles at different times. These roles may be given convenient names which indicate the type of behaviour.

Instructor. This may induce passivity and awe in the students.
Participant. Students need to know when the tutor is and is not using this role.
Model. One of the functions of the leader is to provide an initial model of the conventional language used in a particular discipline or circumstance but it can become theatrical, with the tutor glorying in a knowledge of procedures, systems, criteria, or conventions.
Devil's Advocate. This can be about cleverness rather than wisdom. It emphasizes quick-witted skills.
Neutral Chairperson. It is difficult to use this *and* to instruct.
Consultant. Here the tutor leaves the initiative to the students but makes the range of possibilities clear.

Within these roles there are styles of teaching. For example:

Authoritarian. Tell and sell, teach the facts, demonstrate.
Socratic. Each answer is a trigger for the next question. The tutor only provides new facts *when the trainee demonstrates an area of ignorance.* It is

important to note that if the teacher only provides answers when a particular train of thought (favoured by the teacher) is not followed, then this method reverts to authoritarianism. This style is best for the teaching of reasoning skills.

Heuristic. Action learning by discovery with a sharing of knowledge.

Counselling. This is less directive, and sensitizes students to interactions. Hence its use in teaching interpersonal skills and self-understanding.

Each style may be associated with one role rather than another, the authoritarian style and instructor role tend to go together, for example, but in principle any role could use a variety of styles, and the roles themselves may change during the discussion.

If one observes a group of students participating in a discussion one may get the impression that they are sitting relaxed and with little to do when they are not speaking. The experienced tutor, however, will be aware that for the discussion to be successful there must be a number of activities going on simultaneously in the mind of each member of the group. Each participant must be actively listening; at the same time they are formulating their ideas and possible contributions, they are waiting for suitable opportunities to intervene and contribute, and they have to keep the overall framework and direction in mind. The job of the leader is to enable the group members to cope with this perceptual and intellectual load as easily as possible. Conducting a discussion is therefore a complex procedure, calling for an awareness and sensitivity to the social situation and the needs of the participants.

Perhaps a suitable analogy would be the organization and conduct of a walking tour in a foreign country. The leader of the group has to plan ahead with the aid of maps, guides and other information. He or she will build some variety into the route but will not push the party to extremes which they do not have the experience to cope with. In particular, account will be taken of the varied experience of members. The plan will not be a rigid one; there must be sufficient flexibility to allow for the unexpected and for changes in conditions. It may not be possible to predict the weather, or changes in the route forced by new building or ploughed fields but the aim of the leader will be to have sufficient knowledge of the route to be able to deal with any necessary diversions. At the start of each day the leader will tell the group what the length of the walk will be, the direction, any special characteristics and interesting things to look out for. During the walk he or she may lead from the front in order to set the pace and model the correct way to make the best use of muscles and energy; at other times, however, the leader will go to the rear of the group and leave one of the others to set the pace.

During the walk the leader may decide to take the group on a diversion to see something particularly interesting; it may have been suggested by a colleague, or even another member of the party. The group may decide to look at flowers, herbs, birds and animals, old buildings, and they are likely to discover that among themselves there are a number of people with expert knowledge on these specialized aspects. The leader will decide on time-out pauses for rest and refreshment. As the walk proceeds there will be changes in the character of the terrain and corresponding changes in techniques to deal with it. If the tour is in a foreign country the leader will have a knowledge of the language but will encourage members of the group to try their hand at simple phrases themselves. The leader will be on hand to sort out the problems but will spur on the members to explore for themselves.

The process of organizing a discussion follows a similar path. The leader must plan the session, tell the participants what to expect, and at all times be alert to changes in the situation. A good leader will anticipate problems, but allow the students to act as autonomously as possible, encouraging exploration and an interchange of ideas and information.

In order to help the participants maintain the right approach and environment, the leader may stop from time to time and ask them to reflect on the *process* they are engaged in as a means of carrying the discussion forward. One of the problems of balance which the leader has to solve is to keep the group within the bounds of relevance while at the same time allowing open-ended creativeness. One way of doing this is to avoid overt evaluation. The discussion must always be open in as many ways as possible, including the possibility of being open-ended, that is, allowing it to finish without drawing final conclusions. On the walking tour there is, after all, no need to summarize the experience; it is the experience of the walk which is itself the goal. This of course rejects the idea of summarizing conclusions, but not however of summarizing the course of the argument around the ideas that have been put forward.

In many ways the role of the leader is the administrative one of controlling the traffic – the role of a chairperson. It will be necessary to dovetail a multitude of different approaches, like the traffic at a roundabout. An over-dominant chairperson acts like a centralized control which is less effective than working in parallel. The leader does not take part in the discussion but makes the principles of procedure clear, seeks approval from the participants and ensures that they keep to the procedures. It is important to avoid manipulation.

Leaderless groups

When one first considers a group without a leader it seems to imply a hopelessly muddled and inefficient activity. On thinking about it, however, it can be seen that there are a number of situations in which this model may operate successfully. For example:

A syndicate with projects and assignments;
Informal sub-groups formed during the main group work;
A group which alternates meetings with and without a leader. The tutor may participate in the early stages in order to give the initial framework. There is also the possibility of jointly led groups.

The leader has ultimate responsibility for the functioning of the group and it can therefore be argued that leaderless groups are less efficient. However, they have certain advantages over the conventional group.

Advantages

- Encourage independence, confidence in speaking, practice in leadership skills, raising problems.
- Allow questions of genuine interest rather than encouraging that of conformity.
- Encourage better preparation.
- Encourage a relaxed atmosphere.
- Allow students to reveal their ignorance.
- Go at the student's pace.
- Give the students responsibility and a variety of experience.
- Make it easier for a student to understand other students' frameworks and language.
- Allow more time for students' contributions because time previously used by the tutor can now be used by the students.

Disadvantages

- Absorption of wrong information because there is no automatic correction of errors.
- Explorations may not be thorough.
- Reduces student/staff contact.
- May leave some students anxious.
- One person may dominate.
- Some dynamic leadership and direction may be needed to keep things going.
- A tutor is needed to model the language of discourse used in that particular situation/discipline.

The position in the curriculum

As has been mentioned before, an emphasis on preparation for paid employment and on the need for good human relationships at work puts a premium on those aspects of small group discussion which enhance personal development and relationships. Industry needs workers who are prepared to take individual responsibility and initiative, who are able to negotiate, and to work cooperatively in small groups. There is little doubt that a well-conducted group activity, such as discussion, acts as a social environment in which the individual can develop and in which relationships between student and teacher can be enhanced. Similarly there are major skills of communication which the discussion group can help to develop. But if leaders are to maintain a clear idea of their role, and the direction in which they wish to guide the discussion, then it is important to establish which are the principal functions and which are the subsidiary ones. There are undoubtedly useful spin-offs such as the development of personal identity and better interpersonal relationships which arise from the use of small groups. The key function of discussion groups in the context of this book, however, is that of academic learning and interactive intellectual learning. Other aspects such as social learning, or counselling or therapeutic groups are really incidental to the use of small groups for learning in the sense that it is used here.

Clearly, therefore, the discussion must relate to the overall curriculum. It is a question of relationship though; not a question of trying to cover a set syllabus. If an attempt is made to cover a fixed block of work there is a grave danger of constraining the discussion by putting too great a restraint on the time available. It is important to ensure that the complete syllabus is covered by other means, such as individual study, lectures, computer-assisted learning and so on, so that the discussion periods may be used in a way which enhances their particular qualities.

Within the curriculum itself, discussion may be used at all stages of learning. The first of a series of meetings may form a useful introduction to the course. Such questions as: 'Tell me what you already know about . . .', 'Why is . . . important?', 'How does . . . relate to . . .?', will provide a good starting point to discover how much students already know, and to reveal their prejudices and biases.

The discussion may be used both before and after formal lectures. Before a lecture it can be used to draw out from the students the areas of enquiry which they want to explore, the background to the problem and the reasons why there is a need to study the topic; after a lecture the discussion can pick up on certain points and follow them further, clarify any misunderstandings and formulate a plan of action to follow up the subject. It may also be used after working on a case study (which itself of course contains an implicit discussion).

It is a good idea towards the end of a course to timetable one or more discussions to identify gaps in both knowledge and understanding. This is also the time when a useful assessment of the course itself can be made.

The various types of group discussion and the way they relate to other teaching are described below:

Post-lecture discussion: This assumes that the material from the lecture has been remembered but one can use specially prepared material in order to reinforce the memory. Post-lecture discussions are useful as a check on misunderstandings or insights. There should be preparation time allowed at the beginning of the discussion, or at the end of the lecture to enable students to identify the problems they wish to discuss. There is bound to be a certain amount of tension between the needs of the individual students and those of the group but this is a question of balance. One can either collect problems at the beginning or deal with each one as it is given. The tutor will no doubt have a contingency plan, but revealing that too early encourages passivity.

Step-by-step discussion: Alternate tutor input with a problem or activity. This gives variety and structure and develops skills. The leader must give very clear objectives for this type of session.

Student seminar paper: This should be prepared as a draft, not finished or formal. It should include questions the student wants to ask; these can form the basis of discussion. Students should be clear about what their role becomes after giving the paper or else there will be confusion between tutor and student. There is always a danger that the seminars may become a dialogue between the student and the tutor. One option is to ask the presenter of the paper to chair the session.

Mini-presentation: As above, but not read. This, and indeed the previous type, may be organized with different members of the group performing different tasks – questioning, summarizing, etc.

Springboard (trigger) event: This is a presentation of a (very) short video or other stimulus which raises an issue in concrete form. It may take the shape of a patient asking a doctor's opinion, or someone asking someone else to break a confidence, for example. The group then uses this as a jumping off point for discussion.

Problem solving: This can generate considerable tension and excitement. If the tutor wants to defuse a controversial situation it is possible to take the sting out of criticism by symbolism – students show a green card for agree, red for disagree, yellow for wanting to take over the presentation.

Group event: Case studies, watching a video, conducting an experiment, role-play or simulation.

Group record: Students may be asked to keep diaries, time logs, or other accounts of their experiences. They may be asked to conduct a survey or track down certain information.

Uses

Discussion is widely used in a general way as a finishing or rounding up event in order to ensure that misconceptions are corrected and to provide a forum for an exchange of views and knowledge. In the course of discussion however a number of skills and other benefits will accrue. The following sections give some idea of the potential educational functions performed under the following headings:

- Intellectual and professional skills;
- Communication skills;
- Self-development;
- Assessment;

- Revision;
- Decision–making;
- Creativity.

Intellectual and professional skills

Taking part in discussion teaches the student to think, to set cognitive objectives, and to analyse, evaluate ideas, derive new concepts and apply logic to problem solving. This latter skill is discussed more fully in Chapter 6 together with the techniques for selecting and evaluating evidence.

Apart from the formal aspects of assessing evidence, discussion helps the student to develop the ability to use informal, subjective appraisal, and judgment. It also encourages the mutual interchange of experience and knowledge in reciprocal learning.

In the course of discussion the participants find that they have to defend their judgments against criticism and use their best persuasive powers to convince others of their arguments. This is a subject we shall return to in Chapter 7.

Although the emphasis in discussion is on mutual interchange, there is always the need to base argument on facts. Students may be encouraged to find and use facts by starting with some books readily available but on short loan from a convenient library (after the return of these books the students will more readily use the library for their researches). This preparation will also encourage and help the students in all their handling of information, including statistics and calculations.

Communication skills

As has already been mentioned, taking part in discussions helps to develop oral skills and the techniques of various forms of discourse. Those of argument are dealt with in Chapter 6, those of persuasion and refutation in Chapter 7. There are also the more general skills of explanation and response as part of the process of sharing information and attitudes together with the ability to clarify one's ideas and articulate them clearly.

Part of the means of integrating into a group discussion must be the ability to listen and observe in order to understand the implications of what is going on. The techniques of listening are covered in Chapter 5. The corollary of listening and developing understanding is the use of questioning to probe details and this is discussed in Chapter 4. Implicit in this is the development of evaluation criteria on which to base judgments. Having made an assessment, it will often be necessary to write a report on the meeting and this in itself is a good discipline to learn how to take notes and write such reports.

Self-development

The discussion group also has a role to play in the individual's self-development. It is an opportunity to share and explore different perspectives, to change one's attitudes, and to adjust one's opinions. It is an opportunity to look at the world through other people's eyes in order to adapt your communication to their framework of reference. Working with others also encourages the student to develop his or her own framework of moral values.

The practical experience of working in groups enables students to learn about the other people in the group and about human behaviour in groups generally. It promotes group cohesion and the ability to work closely with others. Because the participants become more aware of each other's views, individuals find themselves more able to admit to gaps in their knowledge and hence are more able to learn from others. This in turn promotes self-confidence and self-awareness and an ability to manage one's own learning.

Assessment

Discussion can be used for assessment. Not necessarily in a formal way, but just by listening the teacher or trainer can see how much has been learnt and understood. It provides feedback on how well previous work has been learnt.

Revision

Revision tends to be one of the most boring and soul-destroying parts of education and training. By using the motivational strengths of discussion, which everyone tends to enjoy, it is possible to consolidate learning, particularly the learning of new concepts and new terminology.

Decision-making

The taking of decisions in a group situation leads to committee-like structures. It is useful for students to have experienced these formal structures and the way they are managed. In particular they can be shown how the processes of consensus-seeking and compromise play an important part in the activity, together with the vital component of time management.

Creativity

The group discussion can be a great source of creativity in which new ideas are generated, relationships synthesized, and speculation encouraged by lateral thinking.

Problems and special techniques

This section looks at some of the problems commonly encountered in running discussion groups and offers some thoughts as to how these problems may be overcome.

Unwillingness to speak

The tutor should:

- Be aware that the students' social and educational background may inhibit them;
- Practise self-restraint;
- Start with topics of general interest rather than the specialized or technical subjects;
- Involve students in choosing what is done, eg arranging the order of topics;
- Be aware that the silent students may nevertheless be mentally active.

Problems such as silent or over-talkative students are best dealt with by acquiring the ability to perceive what is going on without apparently obsessive observation.

Note the danger of disrupting thought processes by interrupting. Research findings show that 25 per cent of the total group discussion time is silence but it is not common to have more than 30 seconds silence at a time. Students soon learn that the tutor will intervene with the answers rather than allow a lengthy silence; this can encourage them to leave the initiative to the tutor.

A tendency to limited, constrained discourse

The barriers to open discussion are both externally imposed and self-imposed. The former are physical constraints, intellectual limitations and psychological and social limits. The latter phenomenon of self-censorship comprises those aspects of ourselves that lead to self-consciousness, and embarrassment.

In order to deal with the self-imposed constraints great efforts are needed to produce an 'enabling' atmosphere, in order to develop better relationships. However, it is not always necessary to iron out personal relationship problems. It is equally important for students to see that it is possible to be in strong professional conflict at work but to be friends outside the boardroom or workplace. Students must learn to separate personal and social problems from work, and rather than shelter them from the chill wind of interpersonal discord it may be more effective to develop a capacity to set aside personal loves, hates, jealousies, fears and interpersonal anxieties and affections except in so far as they are directly relevant to the discussion. Participants must be encouraged to commit themselves in public even if it brings scorn or ridicule on them. Prudence can be inhibiting. (One may have to start with supportive groups until members have built up sufficient confidence, in the same way as children grow away from the family.)

Thus the discussion should be task-orientated and formal in the sense of following rules; otherwise there is a danger of losing the advantages of rational judgment and criticism. Setting clear criteria of how the quality of argument, judgments and opinions are to be assessed avoids the personal aspects of criticism and makes it that much more acceptable.

Not only is open discussion more creative but there is an ethical aspect about concealing truth from others in a discussion. The real problem is that the other participants do not even know that anything has been concealed from them.

Misplaced loyalty can stifle criticism if it is stubborn and resistant to change. This is an aspect of 'groupthink' which is looked at in Chapter 5, 'Listening and the Active Student'.

The 'non-conformer' and anxiety

Having someone in the group who doesn't conform to convention:

- Physically prevents discussion;

- Generates fear and anxiety;
- Provides no common language or points of reference;
- Encourages a refusal to listen – this is the greatest danger of all. It does not so much matter what he or she says, but if we ourselves are denied a hearing that forecloses discussion. As one author put it: 'Open discussion and the open society are threatened I think less by what people might say than by what they might refuse to hear' (Bridges, 1979).

The non-conformer can, however, be a useful asset as a stimulus to the group provided that the group itself feels secure. To encourage members to feel safe, good contributions should be rewarded. It also helps to reduce perceived risk if the leader clarifies the situation, keeps within the group capabilities, and avoids indulging in 'putting down' behaviour for the sake of self-aggrandizement. Members of a group often feel exposed if they feel they are likely to be suddenly called upon to contribute. They can be reassured if the leader asks students to make a note beforehand of the points they may want to raise.

The tutor can use a variety of procedures to help stimulate interaction. Buzz groups give privacy and at the same time enforce participation; students cannot use normal ways of withdrawing (doodling, reading, dreaming . . .). Other methods are the 'cross-overs' described earlier in this chapter, or the 'fishbowl', where half the group discusses, the other half observes, and they then swap over.

Sometimes there may be an increase in the general temperature of the discussion as two or more people start to argue in a more heated way. There is nothing to fear from argument as long as it is conducted within agreed boundaries. It is worth noting, however, that *real* disagreement rather than apparent disagreement occurs when two people understand a question in exactly the same way, but give incompatible answers. Often what appears to be an unresolvable argument turns out to have been an argument about the meaning of words rather than anything substantial.

Danger of alternating student and tutor

One of the greatest dangers is to allow a discussion group to degenerate into a series of dialogues with the tutor and individual students. In order to avoid this happening, the leader or chairperson should not allow themselves to respond to each question but should either store it for future response or turn it back to the group to answer. This technique can be used with great effect when there is a visiting speaker, or even more so where there is a panel of speakers. The tendency is always for the speakers to answer each question and show that they are capable of a quick response. This can be disastrous to the meeting or discussion group because it degenerates into a one-to-one discussion with everyone else left on the sidelines. If questions are stored up for future consideration, or if the group is asked for its opinion, this danger can be averted.

Non-verbal signals are useful in this situation; the tutor can glance round the room during a contribution from a student in order to spot potential contributors. When the speaker has finished the tutor should try not to be looking at them, but at some other part of the group so as to encourage others to take up the running and not to look as if a response from the tutor is going to be immediately forthcoming. It is also useful to indicate the next speaker in a non-verbal way, eg by gesture rather than vocally. This has the effect of keeping the tutor more in the background than if his or her voice is constantly heard punctuating each contribution.

Some contributions may, of course, be rather weak or downright wrong. It is tempting to step in quickly here to keep the discussion on the rails but one should avoid rejecting or correcting contributions, particularly the first ones. It is better to ask for further evidence or turn the point back to the group. At the same time it is important to avoid rigid statements of your own opinions; it is better to be seen more as a devil's advocate or *agent provocateur*. Above all the tutor should try not to answer questions that other students could answer.

A useful technique used by some tutors is to call 'time out' to allow the group to discuss the discussion process. In other words, the group leader tells the group that they are to stop discussing the subject which is before them and instead to take, say, 15 minutes to compare notes about the way in which the discussion itself has progressed and any ways in which its effectiveness could be improved.

The skills of discourse

Students may need to learn the skills of conversation, for example how to intervene by anticipating the end of the previous speaker's contribution. They need to learn to note the use of end-marking phrases and signals; the slowing down of syllables, exaggerated pitch change, body relaxation, use of 'finally', 'this shows . . .'. Conversely there are indications of a desire to speak: body tension, intake of breath, catching the speaker's eye.

In theory the ideal discussion is conducted in a linear fashion and flows from one subject to another in a logical way. In practice there are problems in achieving this type of linear discussion because students hold on to ideas until too late, or get in a muddle because they introduce all their ideas at once. The problem is that while the participants appear to be sitting passively listening they are actually carrying out a number of functions simultaneously, as was indicated earlier. It is not surprising therefore that students often forget the points they intended to make.

A consequence of this is that the discussion narrows down instead of drawing on a wide range of views and ideas. Some of the suggestions already made will help to relax the students and avoid this regression. Students can be encouraged to write down notes and points as reminders. They can be placed in pairs or small groups; in that situation every student has to speak and they cannot be 'outvoted' by a majority. If they are paired within small groups the more nervous members will have the support of their colleague from their pair. The main group then starts to function as a 'report back' platform for the ideas that have been formulated in the smaller groups.

While considering the support given by the tutor to the nervous or timid student it is worth noting that tutors often have a right-hand or left-hand bias when scanning the group – they need to be aware of this and correct it. There is also a tendency to look over the heads of students which is more appropriate to making speeches (although even here it is only of use for novice and nervous speakers).

General points

Where appropriate tutors should check their understanding of a student's contribution by rephrasing it in their own words. However there is a specific problem which is attached to this idea because the tutor's words then become the authorized version. It is worth watching out to ensure that this does not happen to any significant extent. Certainly one should always try to state another person's position in a manner that they approve. One way of ensuring that this is done is to make a rule that everyone must first restate the ideas and feelings of the speaker accurately and to the speaker's satisfaction before giving their contribution. This cannot be sustained for long in practice because it is so time-consuming, but it is a handy stratagem to use on occasion.

The learning of the student in a group situation will be largely mediated by the atmosphere, the environment and culture represented by the group. It is the responsibility of the tutor to ensure that the environment is conducive to learning by setting an example to the students. If the setting is to be informal, for example, then the leader should make it clear that the convention of speaking through the Chair is inappropriate. If students' contributions are to be taken as seriously as the tutor's, then the tutor should be taking notes of their contributions as much as they will take notes of the tutor's. It can be made clear that responsibility for conducting some parts of the discussion is allocated to other members of the group. Tutors should be seen to admit to ignorance and uncertainty when something new arises that happens to be outside their knowledge and should set a good example by stating the connections between their contribution and the general discussion; not everyone will pick up implied connections unaided. They should summarize frequently and repeat points that may be obscure or have been missed.

As with all enterprises, it is helpful to maintain variety and to avoid falling into any one set of habits. Formats can be changed occasionally to keep interest and attention. Using case studies, role-play or going into buzz groups to consider a point can reactivate the dormant energy of the group. There are certain implications in this, however; in the first place it will be necessary to allow sufficient time for variations in pace and activity (at least two hours for any given session), in the second place it argues for an extended series of meetings to allow enough time for any particular activity.

If there is disagreement, it is important to establish the grounds for it. It may be due to incorrect facts, missing facts, fallacious inferences, or incomplete reasoning. At any rate it should be possible to agree on universal principles, from there it is best to proceed to general rules or policies, and only when those have been agreed to continue on to particular cases.

Some ground rules

Mention has been made of the need to establish some accepted rules of procedure. The following are only intended to give an indication of the type of rules that might be applied. They are not intended to be in any way prescriptive.

1. Limit contributions to 30 seconds.

2. Wait 3 seconds after each contribution.
3. No one contributes until he or she has accurately reflected the immediately preceding contribution.
4. No one speaks for a second time until everyone has spoken.
5. The tutor only speaks in response to direct questions.
6. The group takes responsibility for summaries, direction, time-keeping, etc.
7. 'Time-out' may be called at any time.

It is useful to bring short notes or discussion points to read at the beginning of the session and to discuss the goals and objectives of the session at the start. To be effective the goals should be desired and attainable by the students. They should be properly agreed in order to get the full commitment of the students; objectives and tasks must be made explicit, written down in detail and negotiated with the group. Unfortunately there is a corollary to this because there is likely to be resistance to changing goals once agreed, even if the old ones are shown to be unattainable or inappropriate.

Conclusion

Some of the factors which encourage success are:

- Showing confidence. 'We're going to do this' rather than 'Let's try this';
- Using easy questions – not deliberate 'trick' ones;
- Explaining ideas and methods beforehand;
- Training the students in active listening/attentive listening;
- Insisting on keeping to the conventions, eg sharing information, not interrupting . . .;
- Using non-verbal encouragement; ensuring that students' expectations are acknowledged and met.

One should remember that students expect that discussion will be of use to them in their learning; they have every right to that expectation. Discussion is a powerful and penetrating technique and in order to use it effectively the tutor must be prepared to put in considerable effort and skill to enable students to participate fully. Together, students and tutor will be able to achieve far more than either of them could do on their own.

3. Debriefing

Introduction

For the past hundred years or so the emphasis in education and training has been on techniques of teaching rather than on the learning process. When one starts to look at the learning process it is quickly apparent that apart from the mechanical rote learning of facts it is experience that informs us and teaches us how to use the mountains of information now at our disposal.

According to Kolb (1984), learning is the process whereby knowledge is created through the transformation of experience. It is best facilitated in an environment where there is a dialectic tension and conflict between immediate concrete experience and analytic detachment. We learn by seeing and doing things which we then think about afterwards. He expands on this by going on to say that it is characteristic of humans that they learn to adapt to the physical and social world by interaction, reflection, analysis and dialogue: in other words by an extended process of trial and error together with questioning.

Right across the fields of education and training there is an increasing emphasis on experiential learning by means of field placements, projects, structured exercises, role-play, simulations, games, training schemes, case studies, action research and discovery learning. There is a turning away from credit hours as a means of measuring the amount of education that has taken place and towards competence, working knowledge, and information pertinent to jobs. Increasingly we are realizing that students must acquire the ability to form relationships in the family and take responsibilities in the community. The way we learn such matters is to assimilate our experience into our concepts or schemas.

Experience is not what happens to you, it is what you do with what happens to you. In Kolb's model of experiential learning, reflection or reflective observation is the process which provides the crucial link between experience and that process of change and adaptation in the mind which integrates elements of the experience into the conceptual framework of the learner. It is the equivalent of the process used by young children when they talk through and discuss the solution of a problem with other children, or adults, or have a dialogue with themselves or imaginary companions. The process is assisted by promoting discussion of the experience in order to raise to the surface the thoughts and embryonic ideas of the students.

Debriefing is a process whereby students are enabled to make the best use of the experiences which experiential learning techniques give them. It is the time during which much of the learning takes place and yet it is often dealt with on a very casual basis or ignored altogether. The experience of taking part in a structured exercise or role-play, or of having worked on a case study or project needs to be reflected upon and analysed in order to make the most effective use of it. Experience itself does not guarantee growth. Growth occurs when people recognize, articulate and reflect on the feelings that are a result of experience.

The historical roots of debriefing lie in military campaigns and spying. Debriefing is the process which takes place after a mission or exercise when participants are brought together to describe what has occurred, to account for the actions that have taken place, and to enable the development of new strategies as a result. The use of the term has been expanded from its restricted military sense to cover a much wider range of functions. It no longer implies an initial process of briefing because unforeseen situations may be 'debriefed'. Furthermore the purpose of debriefing is now taken to encompass the emotional and psychological needs of the participants as well as their superiors' need for information.

At the very least a good debriefing reduces the chances of being misunderstood; it also provides the tutor with an opportunity to obtain feedback on the success of the exercise. One function of debriefing is to cover information which should ideally be built into the initial briefing, for example the objectives, items to be learnt, assumptions and conventions. Sometimes these cannot be covered in the original briefing. Another purpose of debriefing is to deal with problems which arose during the exercise, and in particular to deal with any 'hidden agenda': unspoken prejudices and assumptions which reveal themselves only in the choice of words or arguments.

One of the difficulties about debriefing after a structured experience such as role-play or simulation is that active experience is involving and interesting, even exciting. Debriefing means the cessation of this activity and the deliberate decision to analyse, appraise and reflect upon it, which by its very nature is not such an exciting or appealing idea. Often it is difficult to stop an activity and encourage participants to begin the debriefing phase. To accomplish debriefing successfully there must be a strong commitment by the group leader to its importance, and this commitment must be transmitted to the participants, which is not always an easy task.

This chapter will deal mainly with the debriefing of experiential exercises such as simulations and role-play because these are the situations which have the greatest number of potential problems associated with them. The techniques are applicable, however, to less emotionally involving situations such as case studies, projects and training schemes.

The purpose of debriefing

The brief introduction above has touched on some of the broad purposes of debriefing, but the picture is much wider than that. It is useful to consider the full breadth of the canvas because that provides a guide to ways in which the debriefing itself should be carried out.

The first objective of debriefing must be to return to the experience and clarify what happened on a factual level. Many things may have been happening simultaneously, and each student will have seen a different aspect of the situation. If it is a simulation, for example, some students may have belonged to one group and others to another group. If the activity was some sort of work experience then perhaps the student may only have seen the work of a small part of a department. The debriefing session is an opportunity to gather these observations together, assemble the pieces of the jigsaw, and obtain information to fill in the whole picture. In the process of clarifying what actually happened any misunderstandings and mistakes can be corrected. It is an opportunity to identify gaps in the students' knowledge.

Although it is important to check on the factual aspects of the exercise, it is equally important to deal with emotional aspects and to ask how participants felt and now feel about it. One of the reasons for using experiential methods of teaching is to encompass the emotional and psychological aspects of behaviour as well as the more physical and factual elements. The exercises are often designed so as to make the student more self-aware and sensitive to others. This process may generate tension and anxiety, and the debriefing session is the ideal time to deal with these outcomes before the student returns to his or her normal course of work. It is also the time at which assumptions, feelings and changes of attitude which occurred during the run can be brought out for examination and analysis.

A special aspect of looking at the emotional side of debriefing relates to debriefing after using role-play. If the student has been asked to play the role of a police officer, for example, and has been subjected to various stressful situations and decision-points during the role-play, then it is necessary to bring the player out of the role in a controlled way. At first it is helpful to ask players to remain in their state of mind as, say, a police officer, and to relate what happened as it happened from their point of view. Only after this has been done is it possible to move away from the singular point of view and look at the overall situation from a variety of viewpoints. Players are often confused after a role-play as to whether they are speaking on behalf of the character they played, and seeing the world through their eyes, or whether they are standing outside the simulation and making an objective analysis. The debriefing process must provide a controlled environment in which the players can both look at the way in which the action has affected them in their roles, and then in an equally controlled way enable them to step outside the roles and become themselves as students or employees once again.

One outcome of the process of looking at what happened and the way in which it affected people is an opportunity for students to develop observational skills, both for watching other people and studying group behaviour, and also for developing the skills of self observation. A well-conducted debriefing session will encourage them to share these observations and teach them some of the techniques of monitoring to use in the future. It provides an opportunity to make them more aware of what is going on both overtly and covertly around them.

Once the debriefing begins, it is natural that both tutor and participants will start to look for connections between the outcomes and the original aims of the exercise. Ideally the initial briefing will have covered such things as the objectives of the exercise, what is to be learnt, the assumptions that are being made and the conventions being followed. Unfortunately it is often difficult to build everything one would like to into the initial briefing, because it would make it too long, it might reveal critical pieces of information too early and some of the information might not be understandable anyway except within the context of the simulation or exercise. On top of that, as every tutor or facilitator knows, simulations and experiential exercises have a habit of going off in their own unpredictable directions. It is useful therefore to have the opportunity to relate aims and outcomes at the end of the exercise.

Having established the facts of the situation and the feelings of the participants, it is possible to build on this information to evaluate what happened, analyse why things happened that way, and hence to draw conclusions about the causes and forces which mould human behaviour. This is part of the general learning which takes place and which can be reinforced or corrected by the teacher or trainer as the discussion takes shape.

Finally the tutor can assess where the group has got to, draw out new points for consideration, and encourage students to consider the implications of what they have learnt from their experiences and how they might apply this learning to other situations. This should be part of a general curriculum plan which integrates each experience into the framework of teaching and learning so that past, present and future learning are seen as part of the same overall structure.

As can be seen, there are a number of different objectives to be achieved, and stages to go through in a suitably planned debriefing session. These sessions are often rushed through lack of time, and not properly prepared. The general attitude is sometimes, 'Well, we've finished work, now let's have a chat about it.' This ignores the need for a purposeful learning session integrated with the overall teaching plan. The advantage of a properly prepared and structured debriefing session is that time is used far more effectively, it ensures that everyone has the opportunity to participate, and it guides the students towards the teaching objectives. This is particularly so with inexperienced groups. The more unaware, inarticulate and uncomfortable the group is, the more structure you need to provide.

It is interesting to realize that the outline structure implicit in the above description is equally applicable to such situations as the debriefing of hostages, a routine which sadly had to be employed many times in the 1980s. The stages can be described as:

Deroling: a need to help the hostages gradually move away from a self-image of victim towards the image of self which existed before the hijack.

Expression of feelings: a clear need to allow hostages to vent their feelings in a neutral and tolerant environment.

Establishing what happened: each hostage will experience the event from a different viewpoint. Each must be asked to describe his or her own personal experience.

Establishing why it happened: it is important to try and establish the causes of these events so that lessons can be drawn for the future.

The remainder of the chapter will therefore lay considerable stress on the need to structure the session and prepare it with the same care as any other learning experience should be prepared.

The logic of debriefing

The three stages of debriefing are:

- to establish the facts;
- to analyse the causes of the observed behaviour;
- to plan future learning or action.

Alternatively one can look on it as a process of collecting data, developing patterns or concepts, and deducing abstractions or principles.

It is often assumed that a debriefing session must consist of one person, the tutor, asking questions of those who participated in the exercise that has just taken place. This is the most common scenario but not the only conceivable one. It is possible to debrief participants in private and individually, or publicly and in a group. The class may be split into smaller groups or pairs to carry out debriefing between themselves. The discussion may be recorded or not, and the amount of structure will vary according to the needs of the group and the tutor.

Using the logic described below the tutor can easily construct a set of steps to be followed in the debriefing session. This can be particularly useful where the group has been divided into a set of smaller groups which undertake the exercises in parallel with one another. In this case the tutor is likely to want a sizable part of the debriefing, or even the whole of it, to be carried out in separate groups since much of it will be particular to an individual group's enactment. This means that the critical job of facilitating the debriefing has to be done by selected students or other tutors brought in for the purpose. It is advisable to give them a clear sequence of steps to follow in order that the maximum benefit is obtained while ensuring that the individuals concerned feel that they have been given a fair hearing and there is no residual stress or strain.

This sequence can be a personal one devised by the tutor. Indeed it is possible to go so far as to write out the exact questions to be asked and have them typed on a set of prompt cards for the tutor or group leader to use. The wording of the questions will naturally vary according to the actual exercise and the needs of the tutor. Most sequences, however, will follow a similar pattern, and the general sequence is illustrated in Figure 3.1. It takes the group through a process of unwinding, reorganizing and crystallizing new pieces of learning and future plans. This corresponds to the general process of any change described by social psychologists as the unfreezing of behaviour patterns, moving to new patterns and refreezing the new patterns into place.

Clearing up – establishing the facts

When a new computer program is used there are often unexpected results due to the complexity of the program, and the unanticipated reaction of one part on another. The process of correcting these mistakes and ensuring that the program functions as it is supposed to do is called debugging. The first stage of debriefing can be regarded as a debugging process. All the incidental dross, mistakes and misunderstandings need to be cleared up and the facts clearly established.

The tutor needs to find out how players saw themselves and others, the impact of various conversations and vocal exchanges on the way people saw the situation. In exercises where there are observers this is the point at which these observers can be asked to say what they observed and to form a picture of the event. Some simulations are undertaken in order to give the students the opportunity to practise skills and procedures which have been taught earlier. These may range from the way in which a receptionist deals with a customer or client, through the teaching of catering students the conventions of serving food and wine, or training clerks in the correct method of filling in

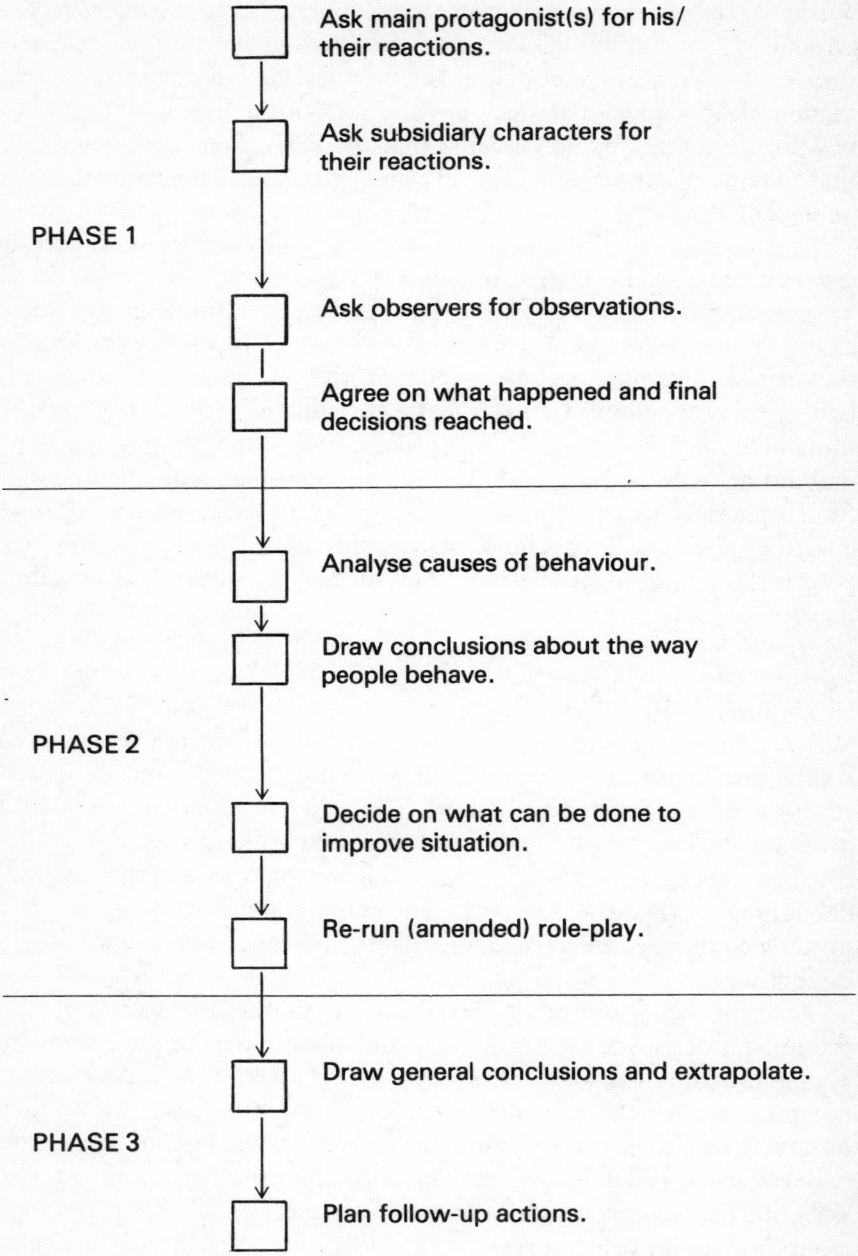

Figure 3.1 *Flow chart for debriefing*

forms, to training in emergency procedures used in the case of a major chemical or nuclear accident. In these cases the debriefing process will largely rest on feeding back observations of the extent to which the student followed the correct procedures. This can be done with checklists, video, observers' notes or other semi-mechanical means. There will still, however, be a need to cover some of the other, more subjective, aspects of the experience.

At this stage one is trying to interpret the actions of the participants in terms of the role-play assumptions. If, for example, one of the students is asked to play the role of a teenager, and the assumption is made that this teenager has a number of friends who take drugs, then one must look at the words and actions of the teenager and their parents in the light of this knowledge. The persons playing the parents might have felt a justifiable (in their eyes) concern if their child insisted on staying out late. The person playing the teenager might have felt a justifiable (in their eyes) frustration at the restrictions placed upon them. The actions of parents and child must be interpreted from the assumptions that come out of the particular personal knowledge, experience and attitudes which someone in their position would have. They cannot be properly interpreted from the standpoint of someone outside the situation.

The clearing up process should also take into account the need to lead the students gradually from the role they occupied in the exercise, towards their role as students, critical observers and objective analysts in the ensuing argument and discussion about the subject under review.

Drawing conclusions – analysing causes

Once everyone has agreed on what actually happened, and how each person saw the situation, the natural question to ask is, 'Why did these things happen how and when they did?' The question is related to the sequence of events, the causes, and what effects were generated. This is the point at which interactions can be investigated and questioned. It is similar to the situation where scientists have observed that two events appear to be connected, and they propose certain mechanisms to account for this, in other words the formation of hypotheses. Just as with the scientists, one can deduce what the consequences of certain assumptions would be and seek to confirm their truth by looking to see what happens in the everyday world.

Suppose for example that someone has reacted strongly to the suggestion that they should work over the weekend. It will be necessary to ask what the background to their objections are, what sort of expectations they had of their job, what social pressures they are subjected to by their family and friends, how short of money they are, and so on. When the group has decided what were the real causes of this problem then its members can look at the way people react in the world outside, and from this perhaps deduce some of the root causes of industrial disputes, family disputes, or problems of recruitment, according to the particular subject that they are studying at the time.

The tutor should draw out a series of these lessons, looking in turn at a number of chains of cause and effect as they are highlighted by the behaviour and reactions of the students in their experiential exercise. From these lessons it should be possible to extrapolate the results into the real world, and to draw generalized conclusions.

Devoloping an action plan

The experienced tutor or trainer will normally have a plan of action to follow at the end of a conventionally planned lesson. The students will be sent away with a summary of what they have learnt, a set of notes, some work to do before the next meeting, and so on. There seems to be something about the use of experiential exercises that tends to encourage the tutor to regard the end of the debriefing as a full stop. Perhaps it is the semi-free nature of the exercise and the unusual amount of talking which is done by the students, perhaps it is the unpredictable quality of most such exercises. In many cases it will undoubtedly be because not sufficient time has been allowed for the debriefing to take place. Whatever the reason, it is often the case that the lesson or session ends at the point at which some conclusions have been drawn about the subject under discussion.

This should not necessarily be the end however. Other exercises can follow from the first, perhaps following the same format but with different parameters. Instead of the father of a normal family being interviewed by a social worker, the mother of a single parent family may be role-played in exactly the same situation. A case study of a large American corporation can be changed by asking what the implications would be for the same situation and financial figures if the corporation happened to be Japanese.

There is also a challenge to the students to suggest how their new-found awareness, knowledge and sensitivity can be put to practical use.

They should be invited to make their own plans to incorporate this new information into their work in the future.

Finally, feedback is also needed on the value of the activities as a whole from the participants' perspective. The tutor or trainer will want to know whether the participants believe that the experience and the manner in which the activities were structured and organized achieved the original purposes, whether the experience matched the participants' beliefs and understandings about the workings of the external world, and whether the outcomes of the experience were useful. They can also be asked how the activities and the debriefing itself can be changed so as to achieve more closely the intended outcomes of the session.

Before leaving the logic of debriefing it is worth emphasizing that the process often takes place after a tiring and stressful activity. The tutor should be ready therefore to offer support with advice and help after the session has finished. In any case the session itself should always end on an upbeat note of relaxation.

Techniques

Debriefing is unusual in discussion situations in that it requires deliberate changes in technique in the course of the session. In addition to following the right sequence, the tutor must also adapt the style of questioning to each stage in the sequence. Both the type of question and the relationship of the tutor and the student must change during the process if it is to be conducted efficiently. Each of these three phases, then, requires a different set of questioning techniques on the part of the tutor. This section looks at these techniques and how they might be used.

There is no suggestion that the changes have to be sudden or abrupt; normally the tutor will move from one to the other in a subtle way unnoticed by the students. On the other hand there should be a definite boundary in the mind of the tutor so that the questioning can change to the most effective form for a particular phase. A summary of these techniques is given in Figure 3.2.

In phase one the emphasis is on the individual role-player. The tutor's role is to keep well in the background. The questioning therefore must be open-ended with ample opportunity for the students to express themselves. There should be no pressure, and silence must be tolerated

Phase 1

Use open-ended questions. How? Why? What?

Concentrate on individual players.

Explore alternative actions.

Reflect feelings.

Insist on descriptive not evaluative comments.

Give feedback in terms of observer's own experience rather than someone else's.

Use group discussion of reaction sheets.

Do not evaluate quality of performance.

Do not argue about misunderstood instructions.

Do not assign motives or make judgements about underlying attitudes.

Emphasize what was done rather than what could have been done.

Use role-titles in discussion, not the player's name.

Phase 2

Ask for reasons. Why? How? Who?

Probe answers. Why not? What if?

Seek alternative theories. Is there another possibility?

Collect other examples. Where else has this happened?

Test conclusions against alternatives. Which makes more sense?

Give views of outside experts.

Phase 3

Get students to commit themselves to actions.

Write up actions on wall posters.

Organize students into action groups or pairs.

Put time scale on actions.

Agree criteria for success.

Figure 3.2 *Techniques of debriefing*

to allow time for thought. Where there is uncertainty or hesitation the tutor can reflect back the statement to the student in the form of a question: 'He didn't seem to be supporting you?' Any comments should be purely factual observations, not criticism or judgment on how well the student has tackled the assignment. It is important not to become bogged down in arguments about misunderstood instructions. If the students acted on misunderstood instructions then it is better to accept this and to discuss what they did in the light of what they thought they should be doing, rather than waste time in recriminations.

Reference has been made to the emphasis which is placed on the use of groups in most debriefing, and to the possibility of carrying out debriefing with the individual. Often the organization of experienced-based programmes involves participants working individually at different sites. Because of this a great deal of debriefing may have to occur between the group leader and the individual student on site, even though there may be a later, larger, group debriefing as well. Rather than being a disadvantage, individually focused debriefing may be extremely effective; on the other hand it is expensive in terms of the trainer's time, and it lacks the stimulation of group interaction.

It is possible to split the group into smaller groups or even pairs for this part of the debriefing and to issue a reaction sheet for them to fill in and discuss in their small groups. Suitable phrases for completion might be:

- I was expecting . . .
- The main problems were . . .
- What helped me most/least was . . .
- Communication was helped/hindered by . . .
- Disagreements were dealt with by . . .

These phrases are completed from the viewpoint of the participants, each in his or her own role. Alternatively a set of questions asking directly for reactions can be used.

Where the debriefing is related specifically to a role-play it is useful to use the role-titles during this phase. This means that students are asked to respond not as themselves, but in the role which they have just taken. Thus one would ask: 'Tell me, as the probation officer, what did you feel about . . .' or, 'Mrs Withers, you were being put under pressure by the headteacher, why did you choose to answer in the way you did?' The advantage of doing things this way is that the student does not feel that you are getting at him or her, but that it is the character whom they have been playing who is being questioned. There is no pressure to put a face on things or to give a socially acceptable answer.

The first phase of the debriefing can be regarded as one in which the participant gives and receives feedback on their behaviour. In this context it is worth remembering some of the basic principles of feedback which experienced group facilitators will be aware of. Feedback should be:

1. Descriptive and not evaluative;
2. Specific and not general;
3. Arranged to serve the needs of both giver and receiver;
4. Directed to behaviour which is capable of change;
5. Solicited rather than imposed;
6. Early rather than late;
7. Checked for understanding by the receiver;
8. Checked for accuracy by outside observers.

One of the ways in which feedback can be given is by using the framework of Transactional Analysis, with a description of the interactions in terms of Parent, Child and Adult relationships but this is not the place to expand on this approach and readers should follow up this for themselves by reading Eric Berne on the subject (1975).

The next phase is one in which the student is asked to come out of the role, the simulation or exercise, and become a student again. This can be helped by physical or symbolic actions such as moving the furniture round to another configuration, removing labels or badges, having a coffee break or some such change.

In this phase the character of the questioning can become more demanding and analytical. The tutor can take command as a person of knowledge and experience. The style of questioning should be aimed at encouraging the participant to make connections with other experiences and with some of the theoretical background to the work. Questions can be direct and closed, ie, 'Should the chairperson have decided in that way?', or 'Which person was effectively taking the role of leader?' As the questioning proceeds the student should be encouraged to look for alternative explanations and examples.

The questions to be asked and the detailed objectives for this phase in the debriefing will depend entirely on the specific needs of the students, the group and the teaching or training task. It is particularly important in phase two to concentrate on the aims of this part of the course and to angle questions and comments towards exploring the issues relating to the subject in hand. This is why generalized lists of questions are only of limited use. The important thing is to ask penetrating follow up questions.

In this phase we are moving from 'inside' to outside and considering what the lessons are and how they might be applied. The tutor can make generalized statements and discuss imaginary situations in order to highlight the key aspects of the lesson.

The third phase, that of getting a commitment to action, may not always be possible but is potentially the most productive of all. It is the phase in which the tutor encourages the students to commit themselves to follow up the experience they have had and to organize further study or experiences which will build on what has happened. Here the emphasis is on getting a public declaration of what they are going to do, with a time-scale to show by when they intend to have done it. They are more likely to keep to their good intentions that way. It is good practice also to agree what evidence will be acceptable to show that they have in fact carried out their part of the bargain.

During phases two and three many of the standard teaching techniques which assume teacher leadership and control can be used. The tutor may want to incorporate illustrative material or expand on certain points. In particular the use of a flip chart to record some of the analytical points made in phase two and the intentions expressed in phase three can be very productive. Not only does it provide a focus for the discussion and a means of pacing the contributions and allowing for natural pauses, it also acts as a record which can be referred to when following up at a later date.

Conclusion

Figure 3.3 provides a checklist of points which are worth taking into consideration when planning a debriefing session.

Effective debriefing requires time. This time must be included in the planning of any experienced-based programme. Too often it is the debriefing phase of a programme which is cancelled or considerably curtailed. Thus the commitment to the importance of debriefing must be accompanied by a commitment to allow sufficient time for a properly structured and conducted session. As a general rule the time allowed for debriefing should not be less than that allowed for the activity itself, and ideally should be at least 50 per cent longer.

1. Allow sufficient time.
2. Arrange room for discussion focused on participants.
3. Ensure each role-player has an opportunity to speak.
4. Check that you have understood the feelings of each person.
5. Keep a written record of points.
6. Draw up list of main conclusions.
7. Consider re-running the role-play with variations.
8. Agree the next step with the students.
9. Make sure that students have understood how their experiences relate to the real world.

Figure 3.3 *Checklist for debriefing*

Most of this chapter has been written from the viewpoint of a debriefing conducted after a simulation or role-play experience. As was indicated at the beginning, it is also good practice to debrief after work experience, but this can be more complex since the tutor was not present to observe and therefore does not know initially what the key learning experiences will have been. It is possible, however, to use records of experience such as students' photos, diaries, time logs, notes, tapes, etc, as a support in the debriefing.

One of the recurrent problems in teaching is that however well-meaning the teacher or trainer is, the teacher talks for most of the time and the students are not able to express themselves and make a sizable contribution to the session. This is the case even where the intention is to allow the session to be student-centred. One of the spin-offs from the debriefing process is that the format makes it much easier for the students to talk instead of the teacher. It is the students who have first-hand knowledge of what went on and they therefore have good grounds for doing a lot of the talking.

There is perhaps one final point worth making. The reader may have got the impression from the above advice that the author is suggesting that students should be kept working strenuously all the time. This is not the intention. The argument is for a more structured and systematic approach to the activity, not for increased pressure on the student. On the contrary, there is much to be said for a certain amount of relaxation and informality during debriefing. The body cannot distinguish between real and false emotion, or between real and pretend crises. If the participants have been truly immersed in the exercise then their minds and bodies will have been subjected to almost as much stress as they would have been in real life. It is quite likely that they will be exhausted and need a period of relaxation before the next job they have to tackle. The ideal debriefing will provide interest, stimulation and relaxation in varying proportions – a challenging and not impossible combination.

4. The art of questioning

The uses of questioning

One usually associates questioning with interviews or, in the extreme, with the interrogation of suspects. A somewhat less stressful and menacing example of questioning is of course the chat show. The techniques of questioning are a key element in such transactions but they can also be fruitfully used in a much wider range of activities. In particular they are a potentially powerful method of teaching.

The idea that a series of questions could form the basis of learning is associated with the names of Plato and Socrates. The so-called Socratic method consists of putting forward a series of hypotheses or statements and propositions and testing them. Socrates asked his students to define the terms they used and showed by giving examples of the application of these definitions how common-sense definitions are often inadequate. From this he refined the definitions and led the students to examine their suppositions by a process of inductive argument, looking at both sides of each proposition, a dialectic self-examination. He showed that by a process of questioning, the students could not only be led to the truth but that they would gain the ability to analyse critically statements made by others in the future.

Socrates developed this use of dialogue as a device which clarified problems by sharpening definitions; he did this by looking at examples and testing the relations between them by the application of logic. He deliberately started by inducing anxiety in the sense that he set about questioning commonly accepted facts, a technique well known to those involved in brainwashing. He then induced the students to think out for themselves the logical consequences of what was being discussed, unlike brainwashing techniques which present ready-made solutions. It is interesting to note that the Greeks used this technique of questioning dialogue in their plays and, through the balancing of question and answer, managed to show both the comic and tragic side of life at the same time, a clever way of ensuring that although the plays were educational they were neither pedantic nor just light entertainment.

Questioning can therefore encourage thinking and a depth of conceptualization. It also encourages the constructive use of talk and helps students to learn from one another. Another of its benefits is to stimulate interest and curiosity and to give students practice in verbalizing their ideas. Asking questions not only helps to monitor learning but in the process of doing so it signals an interest in hearing students' views, particularly if the tutor is skilled in listening.

Questions can, of course, be written down in the form of a questionnaire. This can be a very useful preparation for a discussion period when the results of the questionnaire can be analysed. In the rest of this chapter, however, we will be concentrating on the use of verbal questioning as part of the discussion process itself.

Types of questions

One way of considering questions is to classify them under three broad groups: rhetorical, closed and open. The first of these is strictly not a question at all; it is a statement dressed up as a question, that is to say it is a question which already anticipates the answer. It is a brave person who answers 'No!' in responding to the question, 'Shall we look at the other side now?' Other forms of this type of question are: 'Are we not proud to be . . .?' 'We don't want to disappoint him do we?', and so on. It is really a device for making one's views known while pretending to leave the decision to the listener.

The main classification, however, is really between closed and open questions. In the former case the questioner is providing the audience with a set of possible answers from which they can choose: 'Do you prefer this or that?', 'What time does the next train leave?' These closed questions are characteristically asking for facts, for definitions or names, or for a factual report of an observation: 'What do you call the beam that goes across the doorposts?', 'Tell me what the temperature reading is', 'Who was President in . . .?', and so on.

The open question, as the name implies, leaves the type and extent of the answer up to the other person: 'Tell me about yourself', 'What is the country like?', 'How can we deal with this?' They tend to encourage the respondent to speculate and form hypotheses, to reason and analyse, to evaluate and solve problems. Typically the words 'how', 'why', 'where', 'about', 'explain', 'describe', are used in these questions. This type of question is of a higher order than the closed question and because it encourages the other person to open up his or her thoughts it is the type preferred by counsellors and by tutors who want to encourage their students to think. If you use an open question, however, it is important to make it genuinely open and not to ignore every response except the 'correct' one. It is all too easy to ask 'Give me an example of someone refusing to take responsibility for their actions', and then to say, 'Well yes, but that wasn't the sort of thing I had in mind', or 'Yes, but give me another one.' The experienced teacher will accept the answer given to an open question and build on it.

Another way of looking at questions is to categorize them in terms of their function:

Fact	What is . . .?
Interpretation	What does 'X' mean . . .?
	How would you define . . .?
Value	Which is the best . . .?
Policy	How can we . . .?

or by their structure:

Clear, single *versus* confused, multiple
Asking for recall *versus* asking for creative thinking
Narrow/closed/convergent *versus* broad/open/divergent
Conceptual/evaluative *versus* empirical/factual
Encouraging *versus* threatening

The distinctions between these structures is best seen perhaps by considering some of the ways of wording questions. The following question is typical of the complex questions which one still sees occasionally on official forms or asked by intimidating and unskilled interviewers:

> Do you think that children should be put in the care of the local authority when their parents, or one of their parents, or the person looking after them, behaves violently, or drinks, or is mentally sub-normal, or should social workers help the family to stay together, or does it depend on whether foster parents are available?

It is much better to break down this type of question into a series of single, simple ones. 'Under what circumstances does the law direct children to foster homes?', 'Do you think that parents who drink heavily should be allowed to keep their children?', 'In what circumstances do you think children should be removed from their home?', 'Can you think of any alternatives to removing children from their homes?'.

The wording of a question can be encouraging or threatening, 'Now try and see if you can remember any more', rather than, 'Is that all you can remember?' Some questions may stress the evaluative, conceptual side rather that the factual side: 'What would be the feelings of a parent who is told their child is being taken into care?', 'What criteria should social workers use to determine their priorities?', as distinct from the factual, 'What is the procedure that must be followed before a child is taken into care?'

It is useful to consider various ways in which questions may be categorized because it forces one to appreciate the wide variety of questions that can be used. It is the combination of questions, however, the sequence in which they are used, that has the greatest overall effect, and the next section is therefore focused on that particular aspect.

Sequence of questioning

To watch a skilled questioner or interviewer at work is an exhilarating experience. The questions seem to flow naturally from the answers and yet at the same time the interviewer or tutor seems to be able to control the direction of the process. The secret lies in the sequence of questioning, and it is the ability to have the best sequence at one's command that distinguishes the professional from the amateur in this field. And yet the principles are very simple, and with some practice they can become a natural part of every tutor's skills.

The best sequence of questioning is based on the supposition that although the ultimate purpose of questioning is usually to push the student into new realms of thought, to challenge existing ideas and to probe his or her less openly apparent knowledge, nevertheless it is essential to ensure that there is complete understanding and communication before going on to make demands on the respondent. There is no point in trying to get the respondent to answer questions or analyse problems which are based on misunderstandings.

The way to ensure complete understanding and rapport between the questioner and the respondent is to start from the concrete and proceed towards the abstract. In other words to start with observable real objects or facts and then to go on to hypotheses, suppositions, psychological and social concepts and the like. This corresponds with the classification in open and closed questions discussed above and also the structure sequence of questioning given in the chapter on Debriefing. The sequence will be from closed, concrete questions to open, abstract ones.

The questioner must also be ready to hold up the sequence of questioning for a pause, prompt or probe. A *pause* is an opportunity for the respondent to think about his or her answers and perhaps add some clarification. The questioner may wish to reflect back part of what the respondent has said: 'So you're saying that alloys are in general stronger than the pure metals?', 'You're saying that child abuse is on the increase?' The *prompt* is a device for inviting the student to expand on what has been said: 'Does that have some practical implications?', 'Is that a recent phenomenon, how far does it go back?' *Probing*, as the name implies, is a process of digging deeper and challenging initial assumptions: 'Does that apply to every single alloy?', 'What is the physical structure of the metals which makes that the case?', 'Is child abuse really on the increase, or has our awareness of it increased recently?'

Ultimately it is the searching, probing question which is likely to demonstrate something new to both parties in the discussion. It is therefore worth listing the techniques for probing:

- *Silence*. This is probably the least used and most powerful way of getting someone to develop on what they have said. Observe skilled television interviewers and the way they sometimes use this to encourage further revelations!
- *Encouragement*. A fairly obvious ploy: 'Please go on . . .'
- A request for *elaboration*: 'Tell me more . . .'
- A request for *clarification*: 'What exactly do you mean by . . .'
- A *challenge* arising from the answer: 'But in that case what would be the result of . . ?'
- Asking for *evidence*.
- Asking for a *means of testing* an assertion.
- Questioning *relevance*.
- Asking for *examples*.

Note that these probes can also be applied retrospectively, that is to say they can resurrect something that was said some time ago, either if it connects with what is being said at the current instant, or if the questioner wants to change the direction of the discussion. For example:

'You said a little while ago that some metals formed alloys more readily than others. Can you give me some examples?', 'Do the members of the list we have been discussing have anything in common?'

Whenever using probes, it is best wherever possible to use the respondent's own words so that there can be no argument as to whether you are interpreting them correctly. It is also worth pointing out that probing can reduce the student's motivation and become a mere battle of wits if it is done without sensitivity and without a clear picture of the objectives to be reached.

The reader will probably have noticed the similarity between the points covered above and the interview situation. The interview is after all a particular type of discussion with particular constraints. There is a natural sequence to questioning in the job interview, for example. First the interviewer asks some general questions about background which the interviewee is familiar with. This enables the candidate to settle in. Then there is a sequence of questions designed to fill in any missing details. After that come the more specific questions about skills and experience. After those may follow a few probing questions as to why the candidate wants the job, what appeals to them, why do they think they are particularly suited to it. Finally there will be the closing questions asking the candidate if they themselves have any questions to ask. It is in some ways a ritualistic discussion, and as such is worth studying in its own right.

Problems and pitfalls

The most common pitfall in questioning is the leading or loaded question. The extreme example is the well known, 'Have you stopped beating you wife yet?' It is an insidious type of question because it seems so natural: 'Did you have a good time?', 'Don't you think that . . .?', 'Is everyone happy with that?', 'Tell me why this is a good method'. It is better to angle questions so that they automatically challenge: 'What uncertainties remain . . .?', 'What problems do you see?', 'Give me both the good and bad points . . .'

As has been pointed out before, it is important to ensure that everything is done to clarify and encourage understanding before starting to ask difficult and probing questions. A common technique used by schoolteachers when asking questions in a group situation is to name the person before asking the question so as to alert them to listen carefully. (This is the reverse of the situation where the teacher deliberately keeps the group on its toes by *not* saying to whom the question is addressed until the end.)

The vocabulary used should be simple, and if possible should correspond to the student's own vocabulary. Where the students habitually use slang or vernacular terms the tutor may not wish to use these in discourse but can at least say, 'When I use the term "discourse" I mean what you would call "rapping" or "chewing the fat" . . .', or something along those lines. Where appropriate, terms should be defined before they are used and the context of the question should be explained with examples. Difficult questions should be broken down into their elements or stages.

There should be plenty of relaxed silences in which students can think; a good technique in a group situation is to allow 15 or so seconds after an answer and then to ask everyone if the meaning is clear; if it is not then ask the original speaker for clarification. It is helpful for the questioner to reflect back or rephrase some of the answers in order to test communication and show understanding of how they fit into the joint framework of questioner and respondent. Definitions can be tested by asking for specific examples, descriptions, and processes, a technique which Socrates used a great deal.

The key to successful questioning which enables the student to learn is to be flexible and sensitive. Although it is wise to have an overall plan for the session, you should maintain a flexible approach and vary the questioning to suit the situation. Being sensitive implies, for example, that an apparently irrelevant answer is recognized as a sign that the student may be out of his or her depth, or that the respondent has had to wait so long before getting a contribution into the discussion that it is now out of date. Sensitivity also implies an awareness of the non-verbal body language which reinforces or contradicts what the student is saying.

Finally, here is a list of do's and don'ts which summarizes the best approaches to questioning.

DO	DON'T
Ask questions	Present statements
Ask one question at a time	Ask multiple questions
Ask open questions, funnel (ie start with general questions and proceed to more detailed ones), probe	Ask closed questions (yes/no answers), present forced choices (either/or)
Encourage further explanation	Accept all statements at face value
Ask neutral questions to establish facts	Ask leading questions or loaded questions
Follow leads where appropriate	Change the subject abruptly
Keep an open mind	Make premature assumptions
Keep the questions concise	Ask long complicated questions
Allow time to think and answer	Fire questions in rapid succession
Feedback your understanding and adapt accordingly	Press on with a pre-set series of questions
Listen	Do most of the talking

It is this last point – that of listening – that we take up in the next chapter.

5. Listening and the active student

The need to listen

Up to this point we have been looking at the use of talk from the teacher's point of view. The tutor is not, of course, the only one to ask questions. The students will also want to ask questions, either of the tutor or of each other. Some of the advice in the previous chapter may well be of value to them. But this highlights the transition, as it were, between teacher-centred and student-centred learning. The aim of the discussion is to enable students to express their ideas and beliefs in an open way, and to exchange information and knowledge. The organization of the discussion must necessarily be teacher-centred (unless the students are shown how to organize it for themselves); the actual activity of talking within the discussion is student-centred.

So far we have been concerned to help the tutor to ensure an effective framework for the discussion; the rest of the book concentrates on the techniques which students need to be aware of in order to use oral skills to their best advantage within the context of discussion. The text itself is addressed to the teacher because the amount of information which is appropriate for the student will vary enormously with the particular person or group. Some students will need help and support at a very basic level to encourage them to speak; those who are naturally articulate and from a sophisticated professional background will be able to benefit from the more complex and erudite aspects of logic and argument. It is part of the professional skill of the teacher to select and use those sections which are appropriate to the particular needs of their students.

One of the key skills which must be learnt by students if they are to participate fully in discussion is that of listening. As we go about our daily business we are surrounded by sounds. Even more than in the recent past, we hear music, advertising commercials, traffic noise, and everywhere the sound of people talking. We hear words, we hear speech, we hear conversation; but much of the time we do not listen. Hearing is a physical, passive phenomenon. Listening is an active interpretation of what we hear. It is a process of making contact with the mind of another. Listening can be likened to catching the words and meanings thrown by others. Catching is not passive, it is just as much a positive activity as throwing and it requires as much skill and effort, though of a different kind. Listening requires considerable skill and effort, a reality that is overlooked by many people.

There is today an enormous emphasis on the *transmission* of information. This must be balanced by an equal emphasis on the *reception* system which is needed to complete the process of communication. Just as we have seen that oral communication is a poor relation to the written word, so active listening tends to be treated as the poor relation to speaking, but as has already been pointed out it can be argued that open discussion and the open society are threatened less by what people might say than by what they may refuse to hear. We have lost some of our ability to listen carefully, partly because of innate laziness, partly because we have built up defences against the constant intrusion of noise, persuasion and opinions with which we are bombarded daily.

This was not always the case, neither historically, nor in our own development. Before the days of the printing press, and universal literacy, lectures were read from manuscripts with a commentary and students listened critically and attentively and memorized the principal points for discussion afterwards. The taking of notes became the method of transmission and indeed is still one of the surest ways of focusing the attention. We ourselves before the age of about three learnt a large vocabulary and grammar purely by listening. Since at that age the child cannot read there is nothing to distract him or her from listening and learning. Communication for the very small child consists largely in listening; nevertheless the fundamentals of language and social behaviour are all acquired in this manner. The next stage is that of speech, and it is noticeable that even those who have problems with reading or arithmetic can normally speak well enough to communicate reasonably fluently. After the next step of learning to read however, we become more visually minded and less attentive to speech.

The process of listening

It has been estimated that we spend 70–80 per cent of our working lives

85

communicating; of that time we spend 30 per cent speaking, 45 per cent listening, 16 per cent reading, and 9 per cent writing. Thus we not only learn to listen before we can speak, read or write, but we spend more time in this activity than in any of the others. It is strange then that although we are taught a great deal about reading and writing, and sometimes a little about speaking, we are taught virtually nothing about the skills of listening. This is all the more worrying when one realizes that tests have shown that after a ten-minute talk the average listener has heard, understood, properly evaluated and retained only half of what was said, and that half of what is retained will be lost within the next few hours.

The reason that so little attention is paid to training in listening skills is that it is assumed that it is a simple process and one that can be picked up without training. The truth is that the process of listening is remarkably difficult even at the initial physical level because of the constraints which operate. The physical components of conversation and speech generally consist of a series of short words, phrases and sentences. Surprising as it may seem, in normal conversation half of the spoken words are in fragments of three words or so and three-quarters of the phrases are less than five words long. These are broken up by periods of silence which take up to half of the total time but are relatively short, mostly only a few seconds and rarely as much as 30 seconds. In fact most people talk at the same speed; the 'chatterboxes' appear to talk faster because they devote less time to pauses.

These events (significantly the Hebrew term 'dabar' means both 'word' and 'event') flow through in a continuous stream. The sound which comprises the words exists only as it is already going out of existence. If you stop a video recording you may study the picture as something static, but you cannot capture the accompanying sound in the same way. If you stop the sound you cease to hear it. Even the first part of a word has disappeared before the final part has been received. Luckily the brain can process information far faster than someone can speak, but nevertheless the physics of sound and speech are such that the listener has to concentrate so that the brain can form stable and lasting patterns before the sound disappears. Ironically, this speed of processing coupled with the intermittent silences also means that there is a danger of 'switching off' or running ahead for very brief periods. It is during those periods that we may miss vital information or, even worse, develop our own structure and background instead of following those of the speaker.

Understanding and interpretation

The physical constraints may inhibit the listener from perceiving all that is said; the psychological constraints prevent us from fully comprehending it. Techniques of listening must enable us to catch the whole message which is being sent to us, but they must also ensure that we understand and interpret the messages correctly. In order to do this it is important to appreciate the context of the message and the implications of who the speaker is. One way of doing this is to listen carefully to the tone of voice, inflection and so on.

There are four stages of listening: sensing, interpreting, evaluating, and responding. The first stage, that of *sensing*, consists of disentangling the sound of words from that of background noise. This may sound easy but of course it relies on considerable experience, as any learner of a new language will realize.

We exercise a certain amount of selectivity about what we hear, depending on our current concerns and interests; the remainder is relegated to the background. Most people will have observed for example that they hear their name mentioned even when they have been paying no attention to the conversation, a common experience known as the 'cocktail party phenomenon'. If someone is telling us some news which we would prefer not to hear, we may unconsciously block it out. When we are with our children, spouses or close friends we make assumptions about what they are saying and cease to listen to the detail. Any one of these factors can impair our ability to register content accurately. The only way to overcome the problem is by complete concentration.

The second stage, already touched on earlier, is that of *interpretation*. It is an astounding fact that many of the sentences that people utter have never been heard on earth before. It is therefore not just a matter of recognizing the words, but of interpreting their meaning in the context of the situation. The tragic crash between a KLM and a PanAm jumbo jet on the runway at Tenerife in March 1977 was due to a misunderstood instruction from the control tower. At a more mundane level, people do things, arrive early or late, act quickly or slowly according to *their* interpretation of the meaning of instructions. One of the important aspects of interpretation is that of understanding the difference between fact, inference, assumption and opinion, and distinguishing between them when listening to discourse.

Having understood the message as the speaker intended it, there then

87

follows the process of *evaluation*. There are a host of unconscious assumptions which colour our assessment of messages: the way speakers are dressed, their prestige, previous information about them, and our experience of similar situations. It may even be that our final evaluation is that, 'It's not my problem'. The task of the trained listener is to bring these assumptions into the conscious and to check out that they are reasonable and not interfering with an open mind. This is particularly important in the interview situation.

Finally there is the matter of *responding*. Not necessarily verbally, but responding either verbally or non-verbally in a way that gives some feedback to the speaker. A completely blank face, silence, a cold factual reply, will destroy the relationship between speaker and listener. But it is this relationship that ensures an accurate and easy flow of information between the participants. Without it there will be none of the feedback to correct misunderstandings. A response does not imply agreement; it can be non-judgmental, but without some sort of response the two-way communication will dry up.

Techniques

One of the key techniques when listening is to keep a set of questions in your mind:

- What is this about?
- What are the main arguments being put forward?
- Are the arguments sound?
- What consequences follow?

The danger, as explained above, is that the listener's mind will wander ahead and build up a whole edifice of assumptions. It is best therefore to suspend judgment until you are confident that you fully understand the speaker. In particular it is important to sustain the difference between knowledge and opinion.

One technique for keeping one's mind on the present is to take notes. These notes can be written down or you can make a mental note. In a group situation they can be divided into sections for each speaker and/ or subject area. Particular heed should be taken of opening remarks, they often contain the structure of the argument or case; note should also be taken of the initial premises and assumptions and who made key comments. Problem words and definitions should be recorded mentally or on paper, together with the logical steps which were followed and the conclusions arrived at. When taking notes one should work out the structure of what is being said: determine the key points but avoid noting one's own reactions at the same time – this is placing too much emphasis on one's own concerns. It is useful to imagine that you are going to have to give a report and to plan it even if in reality you will not be called on to do so.

Every utterance has some sort of structure or framework which is either consciously or unconsciously used by the speaker. It is useful therefore to establish this framework for one's own listening. It may follow a pattern of enumerating points, solving a problem, going through a chronological sequence, or drawing a spacial/pictorial analogy. Summarizing the main points, both to oneself and sometimes as feedback to the speaker can be helpful. Both framework and summary can lead to the development of an action plan which can be jointly agreed.

One of the most difficult things in listening is to accept what is said on the speaker's terms and not to force it into a preconceived pattern. One must listen to what is said and not edit it into what you would have preferred to have been said. The other major hazard is that of being side-tracked or lapsing into a day-dream. The brain is liable to race ahead of the speaker and any spare time available should be used to think actively and positively about the ideas expressed; to summarize, evaluate, interpret and respond. A good 'rule' developed by Carl Rogers, the US psychologist, is to restate the ideas and feelings of the speaker accurately and to that person's satisfaction first, before going further with the discussion.

The attitude of the listener is important. One should listen optimistically, judge content and not delivery, and not jump to conclusions. The emotions should be held in check; emotion-laden words should be noted and deliberately put aside. The feeling should be one of a relaxed attentiveness. 'Let the student finish his paragraph', ie allow time to develop thought, rather than jump in quickly with correction, otherwise discussion can become the monopoly of the quick and articulate. There should be plenty of eye contact and non-verbal encouragement. If listening to a group of students it is worth remembering that each of us has a bias towards either left or right in looking at a group, and to correct for that bias. Many lecturers have become used to looking over the heads of their audience and must remember to look straight at the student speaker when listening.

Above all else it is essential to keep the question of listening techniques at the forefront of one's mind. Periodically one should ask oneself, preferably by going through the points raised in this section, whether one's listening is as active and positive as it could be. It is necessary to work at listening, to repeat back what you think you heard, to check, to think, to ask.

Problems

Some of the obstacles to listening arise from the complex physical and mental task which it represents. In the average situation listeners will simultaneously be formulating their own ideas and contributions, waiting for an opportunity to intervene or contribute, and keeping the overall framework and direction in mind.

The brain can only retain five or six items for a minute or so in its short-term memory. It therefore has to be highly selective about incoming information, and place it in a pattern or framework to aid longer-term memory. Once the pattern is established all new information will be edited to conform with this pattern and it is important to question constantly the assumptions one is making. The key question is not, 'Is this how I see it?' but 'Is this how the speaker sees it?'

The actual act of distinguishing words can itself be difficult if the speaker is not clear. Each language selects what differences between phonemes will be important. In English for example the difference between 'bet' and 'pet' is important; in other languages the difference in the sound made by the English 'b' and 'p' would be regarded as negligible. On the other hand Hindi distinguishes between the 'p' sound in 'pin' and 'spin'; if you put your hand in front of your mouth you should be able to detect the difference. Non-native speakers, or dialect speakers of English will therefore present yet another load on the interpretive functions of the brain.

The other blocks to effective listening are mainly psychological. By being aware of them we can attempt to diminish their effects.

Judgment

Although it is necessary to evaluate what is being said, the act of judging will itself interfere with listening to the next item. It does not make any difference whether listeners agree or disagree, in both cases they will be preparing personal arguments to rebut or fit in with the speaker. It is worth noting that this means that the custom of introducing something 'controversial' into a talk does not guarantee that people will listen more attentively – they may just be rehearsing the arguments and counter arguments in their own minds. Similarly if speakers state conclusions at the beginning of their talks the audience will start to consider their own arguments for and against them and cease to listen attentively.

Just as the temptation to spend too much time evaluating the ongoing speech must be avoided, so too should the temptation to allow appearance, behavioural attitudes, mannerisms, tone of voice, and language to cause the listener to 'switch off'. People like the feeling of superiority given by being critical of others' vocabulary and grammar; it is necessary to discard these aspects and concentrate on the ideas and logic of what is being said.

Non-critical inference

It is all too easy to jump to conclusions, particularly in respect of the likely motivation or behaviour of someone of a particular sex, age, social class or ethnicity. The real meaning of each remark must be clarified, if necessary by questioning or restating what appear to be the facts. Recognition of the fact that inferences are being made is at least a significant step towards a solution.

Plural inference

This is the phenomenon of assuming that other people think the same way as we do ourselves. Both speaker and listener can assume that the other is thinking along the same track. In many ways this is actually a great asset because it enables one to fill in the gaps in the conversation. If we hear the words 'She turned from the blackboard. "Come in officer," she said', we immediately make all sorts of assumptions about the location, the speaker's profession, and what the situation may be. This is useful in enabling us to have an informal conversation but in a learning situation we can sometimes presume too much. One way to avoid this is to act as 'devil's advocate' and to question one's own beliefs and assumptions.

Closed mind

The greatest minds have always had a multiplicity of interests. When we read about figures such as Socrates, Copernicus, da Vinci, Benjamin Franklin, Einstein, we discover that they had a wide outlook and open minds. G K Chesterton said: 'There is no such thing as an uninteresting subject. there are only uninterested people.' Voltaire said: 'I disagree with what he says but I will defend to the death his right to say it.' The spirit of curiosity should be encouraged and the listener should feel that everything is worth paying close attention to.

Lack of humility

Students are often reluctant to admit that others may have something to give or that they themselves may be wrong. They do not relish the prospect of being changed. This fear of taking on board something which could affect one's attitude or behaviour must be banished if students are to listen with an open mind.

Environment

It has been said that discussion is a tapestry of speech and silences. In order to create this tapestry and to weave the many strands together one must ensure that people have time to think. There must be a relaxed atmosphere in which silence is acceptable and encouraged. Speakers and listeners should be able to maintain eye contact, the seating should allow for relaxed body posture, and the expectation should always be that speakers have the time and freedom to explore what they want to say. The exploration is a joint one, with the listeners illuminating what is said by clarifying, summarizing and evaluating along the way. It is a matter of teamwork rather than one person imposing views on another. One of the best ways in which listeners can help is by restraining their own natural desire to talk, interrupt or show off their own knowledge. Their turn will come.

Putting together all that has been dealt with above, it may be useful to have a practical checklist of questions for students to ask themselves to see whether they are listening actively:

- How was this contribution introduced? How does it connect with previous items?

- What is the overall structure of the contribution?
- What is the basic argument/question?
- What assumptions are being made?
- Are there any words I do not fully understand?
- Am I forcing my own prejudices on to it?
- Does the tone of voice correspond with the perceived message?
- Am I summarizing periodically, either in my head or by means of notes?
- Have I checked my assumptions/interpretations with the speaker?

We have been considering the need to encourage students to take an active role in discussion, and the way in which listening skills can help to ensure this involvement. A good group of students will build up rapport and will encourage and support each other in their activities. By this means they will be enabled to participate fully and feel that their colleagues are listening and taking note of their ideas and that those ideas are being received favourably. It is largely through this mechanism that every student can be prevailed upon to take part. There is a danger of going too far, however, and developing an atmosphere in which active listening can lead not only to active participation, but also to uncritical acceptance of other people's suggestions. The last part of this chapter is given over to a short account of the phenomenon known as 'Groupthink', which is one of the manifestations of this uncritical attitude.

'Groupthink'

The concept of 'Groupthink' was first put forward by Irving L Janis (1982) in the 1970s. He pointed out that although on the whole it was an admirable idea to work towards group unity and cohesiveness, and that a group which worked as a team operating on a consensus basis was in many ways an ideal to be aimed for, nevertheless there were serious drawbacks which became evident if the committee or group became too tightly bound together. It could lead to bad decisions, failure to look at alternatives, lack of self-criticism and even an attitude which disregarded the personal and human needs of those who were involved. 'Groupthink' arises when the striving of group members for unanimity overrides their motivation to appraise alternative courses of action realistically.

Conditions which predispose towards 'Groupthink'

The conditions in which 'Groupthink' flourishes are those which predispose towards a tightly-knit, inward-looking, homogeneous group. There will be no tradition of impartial leadership, no methodical procedures for ensuring all aspects of a subject are considered, and the members of the group are likely to come from a homogeneous social and ideological background.

The situations which provoke 'Groupthink' responses will be those which induce low self-esteem because of recent failures, excessive difficulties in making decisions, and apparently insoluble moral dilemmas. Under these circumstances the leader's solutions are likely to be seen as offering a good way out

Symptoms

A group operating in these conditions will create for itself an illusion of invulnerability and an unquestioned belief in the inherent morality of the group despite any evidence to the contrary. It closes its mind to outside influences by a process of collective rationalization and self-censorship of deviant views. Outside critics are stereotyped as evil, weak and stupid and ulterior motives are attributed to them which diminishes their influence. There are internal pressures on members who express strong arguments against one of the group's stereotypes, illusions or commitments, and because of these pressures on dissenters people will tend to keep quiet. This produces an illusion of uniformity, silence being taken for consent, which is enhanced by self-appointed mindguards or censors who protect the group from disrupting information.

Results

The major outcome of 'Groupthink' is to diminish the effectiveness of decision-making. There will be incomplete surveys of both objectives and alternative solutions. There is a failure to examine risks and to work out contingency plans. Incoming information is treated selectively; alternatives which have been rejected, however prematurely or precipitately, are not re-examined at any stage. The escape from individual responsibility can lead to inhuman attitudes. 'Groupthink' overcomes soft-heartedness and morality and allows dehumanizing action.

The sense of belonging, reassurance, unity, harmony, peace and strength, may be at the price of intellectual vitality and the advance of intelligence; loyalty stifles criticism unless the participant is prepared to change if the counter evidence is strong enough; it may in other words be misplaced loyalty. Seeking a consensus can obstruct critical enquiry; one should encourage participants to rely on their own standards of judgment.

The common defects in decision-making are as follows:

1. Few alternative courses of action are considered;
2. There is no consideration of objectives and values;
3. There is failure to reconsider the preferred action, to detect non-obvious risks and drawbacks;
4. The group never seriously reconsiders actions initially rejected by the majority;
5. There is no attempt to get information from experts on the estimates of gains and losses;
6. The group is biased in reacting to factual information, and has a bias towards the initially preferred policy;
7. There is failure to work out contingency plans.

In his writings, Janis shows how some American decision-making fiascos such as the Bay of Pigs, Vietnam, Pearl Harbor, can be attributed to 'Groupthink'; he also shows how this can be avoided and cites good decision-making such as the Marshall Plan, and the handling of the Cuban Missile crisis.

Ways of avoiding 'Groupthink'

1. Encourage each member to evaluate critically. Make sure they all have general as well as specialist functions. (But this prolongs the debate and demoralizes the proposers!)
2. Make sure that the leader's original briefings are unbiased without advocating specific proposals. (But then the leader can find him- or herself locked in battle to persuade the others of his or her ideas.)
3. Set up parallel working groups to consider questions.
4. Let each member take the group's deliberations to other groups outside, to discuss and report back to the main group.
5. Invite outside experts or qualified colleagues to attend single

      meetings and encourage them to challenge the views of the core
      group.

6. Assign one member the role of devil's advocate. Use a different member at each meeting. Encourage a more heterogeneous membership of the group. Look at things from the opposite point of view.

7. Hold a 'second chance' meeting at the end of a series where students are encouraged to express residual doubts and to rethink issues. This second consideration should be held in different surroundings and in a less formal way to emphasize the change of attitude.

This brief account of 'Groupthink' will show the importance of striking a balance between developing an enabling atmosphere of trust, and allowing the group to acquire an uncritical attitude.

Having looked at two of the detailed aspects of discussion, those of questioning and listening, we turn now to look at two of the most powerful ways of using speech: argument and persuasion.

6. Argument and debate

The use of argument

Why bother to argue? Well I suppose because we enjoy it, like the rabbi who approached a couple of people who were bickering together and said, 'Is this a private quarrel, or can anyone join in?' But there must be better reasons than that. In fact the process of argument is far more fundamental to human communication than one might suppose. It provides the basis of thinking, it is a powerful method of teaching, it lies at the roots of the democratic process, it supports the development of the individual, and it can encourage the elegant and sophisticated use of language.

This need to revive the skills of debate was commented upon by David Putnam, the film-maker, who said in a lecture to the Royal Society of Arts in London in 1988, that in America the real tragedy was that so much talent and so much wealth was squandered on the second-rate. He went on: 'I think this tragedy begins with a timidity of mind, a kind of intellectual avoidance. For example, in America today it has become hard to find open and honest debate. The sheer joy of the clash of ideas seems to be missing, to have lapsed into disuse. And that cannot happen without collusion from an intellectual community which includes the artist. This ingrained reluctance to debate, certainly in the sense that I understand debate, as the unbridled contest of ideas, has had a fatally enervating effect on everything from art to politics.'

Thinking

The process of thinking almost always involves the use of words; even when mathematical symbols or diagrams and pictures are used they tend to be translated loosely into words for the purpose of thinking. Reading involves talking to oneself, often silently; thinking involves turning this monologue into an internal dialogue whereby one argues the point with oneself. The word 'dispute' itself is related to the Latin 'putare' – to think.

The process of argument does not necessarily imply a fight; it can equally be a cooperative activity, a journey of reasoning together in order to arrive at a logical conclusion. Argument does not always imply antagonism.

Teaching

One of the most important elements in teaching is to encourage the student to work actively at the material to be learnt, to discover a logic in it, and to develop a personal framework for remembering it. A powerful method for doing this is what is nowadays known as 'discovery learning', a method pioneered by none other than Socrates many centuries ago. The Socratic method, which has already been touched on, is that of a process of questioning by which the student is lead to clarify his or her thoughts and to arrive at the truth by a process of narrowing down the options.

Self development and democracy

A healthy tradition and practice of argument encourages a critical spirit in society which develops independence and self-assurance. It is one of the most reliable ways of ensuring a democratic, open society. Socrates said that 'the unexamined life is not worth living'; in other words, life which is not scrutinized in a critical fashion is not worthy of being lived by an intelligent human being. The inculcation of critical argument as a way of thought ensures that people constantly question what they have been told; it makes them more resistant to the blandishments of advertisers and politicians.

Use of language

The English language is an exceptionally rich and subtle one. There are a variety of ways of expressing one's thoughts, each having a particular emphasis and implication. The practice of argument develops the elegant and effective use of language in ways that are greatly superior to writing. The spoken word stimulates immediate feedback and hence is self-teaching and self-correcting. It enables the speaker to add variety in tone and emphasis, and it provides a platform for trying out different approaches in a short space of time without the burden of worrying about the spelling of new words.

Debating

Although this chapter is not intended as a manual to train the reader to argue in a court of law, nevertheless debate is a useful means of developing clarity of thinking as well as of improving one's techniques for putting a case and spotting the fallacies in other people's arguments.

The courtroom is of course the classic situation in which argument takes place. This is an example of formal advocacy and is paralleled by similar situations such as tribunals and boards of enquiry. Parliament and Congress are other examples of formal environment for debate, as are the more structured type of conferences and committees.

Debate can itself follow formal lines and use technical terms. It can follow the rules of logic as explained below, with a series of major and minor premises and syllogisms. It can even follow the structure of the mediaeval disputation with its sequence of presentation, granting of some conclusions, denial of others, and distinguishing between logical cases. On the other hand debate can be no more than the informal argument which takes place in the home, at work, or in the pub.

It is important to realize that, particularly in the informal setting, debate does not have to be adversarial; it can be exploratory, a sharing of different perspectives and a cultivation of empathy on controversial issues. This is highlighted by regarding discussion as fulfilling two possible roles. *Reflective* discussion seeks to engender an understanding of, among other things, the variety of standards and criteria which people have for making judgments. Suppose for example that people are discussing the merits of two paintings. The discussion is more likely to highlight the varying criteria used by the participants in judging a painting, or the past experience they have of looking at paintings and hence their subjective standards, than to use objective, logical argument. If the discussion is, on the other hand, an *argumentative* one then it presupposes that some consensus on procedures whereby judgments can be verified or refuted has already been arrived at. Thus if these people are now going on to discuss whether an art gallery should purchase certain paintings then they must first agree on some fundamental policies about the purpose of the art gallery, the balance between quantity and quality, and the commercial value of the paintings under consideration. Only after they have agreed on such fundamental premises, or starting points, can they apply logic to their argument. Often therefore the major task proves to be that of getting agreement on the facts and criteria for decision-making rather than the actual debate itself. This preliminary discussion or argument will often be one of joint exploration and reflection.

The process of argument

The essence of all argument is to start from widely accepted principles, such as 'All men (and women) are created equal', 'One should always try to avoid causing pain to others', 'We owe a duty to future generations', and then to use logic supported by relevant facts to apply these principles to particular situations. It may be that not everyone is prepared to accept the principles in the first place, in which case one has to go further back until one finds a fundamental statement on which all agree, and then argue forward from that. Even where the principles are accepted, it may be that their applicability to the particular case in point may be questioned.

In this chapter we will be looking at the process, structure and logic of argument, at some of its qualities and uses, at obtaining and testing evidence, the classification of argument, meaning, fallacies, and practical techniques of getting attention.

Structure

The first step in any argument is to define the problem and the scope of the debate. It is at this point that it is useful to define terms and agree the interpretation of ambiguous words. It is also the point at which there should be agreement over facts. This is the stage which in logic is called the establishment of the premises, ie the basic foundation on which the argument will be built. Considerable time can be wasted if both sides make different assumptions from the start; if the original premises are faulty then the final conclusion is bound to be faulty. In theory each contender should follow Plato's prescription: 'He must be purged of his prejudices first and made to think that he knows only what he knows, and no more'. In practice the adversaries are likely to start with a whole suitcase full of prejudices and unspoken assumptions. Students should be encouraged to question these assumptions.

The body of the argument consists of a series of logical statements which lead to the last stage – the conclusion. Fundamental to argument, and thinking, is the human capacity to invent counter-argument. Human perception is built upon contrast; one can only perceive an object by contrasting it with its surroundings. Argument is built upon statement and refutation: two points are placed side-by-side and the contradictions revealed. This process of looking at opposites is known as dialectic. Even where one looks at the process of categorization, a focusing on common elements, there is by implication a parallel process of discrimination in which one is looking for those items which are unique by virtue of the difference between them and items in the same category. Students should be made aware of this process and be taught always to look at both sides of a question, even where in their own opinion the evidence for one side is overwhelming.

Evidence

Part of most arguments is the presentation and accumulation of evidence for the each of the two sides. (There is a Chinese proverb, however, which says that there are three sides to every question – my side, your side and the right side!) The gathering and use of evidence is beset with problems and students should learn how to identify weak evidence by looking at some of the problem areas described here. The first problem is to ensure that the evidence is relevant and not diversionary. Thus if there is an argument about the way in which the government funds the hospital service it is irrelevant and diversionary for someone to say, 'Well, housing is better maintained nowadays.' Still less is there justification for using such disparagement as 'it's old-fashioned'. There are a number of wholly admirable things which happen to be 'old-fashioned'; having been in existence for a given period of time is irrelevant to the quality of the thing in question.

Clearly, an important part of argument is asking for, and presenting, evidence. Perhaps one of the first things to be aware of then is what is genuine evidence. It is very easy to use a tautology as part of so-called 'evidence'; for example to say, 'You must admit that too much exercise can be a bad thing.' Of course too much of anything is a bad thing; that is the definition of the term 'too much'. It does not add to the argument.

Or, for example, 'They are not allowed to do anything unacceptable.' Similarly one must be sensitive to the use of speculation as fact: 'People say that . . .', 'It is obvious that . . .', 'Surely it is undeniable that . . .' This is not factual evidence, it is a hopeful assumption which can be challenged if need be.

Evidence can rarely be first-hand. It usually arises from the reporting of others and to that extent it is important to ask oneself how reliable it is. Is the reporter an expert or authority on the subject? Is he or she a competent observer with opportunity to gather evidence? Is there an in-built bias? Are the statistics out of date? Even where the information itself appears to be accurate, it is important to consider the processing of the information, particularly numerical information. Was the sample a representative one? Are the appropriate units of measure being used? Is the appropriate statistical unit (mean, median, mode, etc) being used? One of the classic errors in the interpretation of evidence is the assumption that because some buildings from earlier ages have stood for hundreds of years that therefore the architects of those periods must have been extremely skilful and understood sophisticated structural engineering. The truth is that most of the buildings fell down after a time; those we wonder at today happen to be the only ones to remain standing.

Even where a connection or correlation can be shown, it may be a spurious one. The Latin tag, *post hoc ergo propter hoc*, means 'Because one thing follows another the first one must have caused the other'; a common assumption but clearly a dangerous one. Most heroin addicts drank milk when they were children; but drinking milk does not lead to heroin addiction. An obvious fallacy, but much more difficult to deal with when, for example, arguing the case about the potential effects of reading pornographic material. Most of those found guilty of sexual offences will be found to have read pornographic material; this does not establish cause and effect.

There are two other potential problems when dealing with evidence. First, the idea that popularity proves something. Strictly speaking the only fact that can be derived from the statement that something is popular is that a lot of people like it. Second, there is the problem of having convincing evidence brought to bear on the wrong question. There is a considerable body of evidence now that there are no ill effects on computer or word-processor operators due to radiation from the monitor. The real question, however, is not whether there are ill effects due to radiation but whether long periods of operating a computer or word-processor can cause ill effects, and if so, why.

When looking at evidence, therefore, it is first of all necessary to look at it in context; is it relevant to the question under discussion? Next it should be checked for accuracy and the real meanings of the findings judged by making enquiries about the circumstances leading to the evidence being available. There should be no subsequent contradiction between two or more pieces of evidence. Finally one must learn to recognize when pieces of evidence are missing or more are required.

Logic and reasoning

Having established some principles and facts which are accepted by both sides, the major part of argument relies on using logic and reasoning to arrive at a conclusion. Textbooks on logic can be very daunting at first sight. One of the reasons for this is that the most logical of subjects is mathematics and it is convenient therefore to use the language of mathematics and its symbols in describing the logical process. The basic principles of logic are very simple, however, and what follows is an attempt to convey to the tutor an idea of some of the basic flaws that one meets in argument, using symbols only sparingly. These ideas can be introduced a few at a time and students can be encouraged to spot the fallacies in their own and others' arguments.

The Greek philosophers are very much identified with logic and rhetoric but it was the seventeenth-century French philosopher and mathematician René Descartes who pointed out the need to pay attention to the preliminaries. He taught his students: never to accept anything as true unless they knew it to be so; to avoid hasty judgments and prejudices; to divide the problem into parts; to work from the simple to the complex; and to review all the evidence at every point.

The two lines of logic which can be applied to a situation are *induction* and *deduction*. Induction is the process of gathering a body of evidence, observing a number of instances and building up a generalization, a probability that something will happen or that something is so. It is a consolidation of all the information that has been gathered. Deduction, on the other hand, is the process of starting with what has already been found out and accepted as true or probable and leading on from there by going through a series of steps to arrive at a logical conclusion. It is a question of starting with a set of principles or laws or facts, which are

103

known as the premises, and using a series of logical steps or proofs, known as syllogisms, to conclude the consequences for a particular instance.

Syllogisms are often expressed for convenience in the shape of mathematical equations like the following:

> All Xs are Y
> Z is an X
> Therefore Z is a Y.

In other words:

> All cars are road vehicles
> A Ford Fiesta is a car
> Therefore a Ford Fiesta is a road vehicle.

There are many variations and rules that are generated by studying these syllogisms. For example you cannot deduce anything from two negative premises. To say that John is not a driver, and that Mr Smith's name is not John, does not tell us anything at all about whether Mr Smith is a driver or not. Similarly the meaning of words must not change in between premises; This is what lies behind such paradoxes as:

> A piece of dry bread is better than nothing
> Nothing is better than a good meal
> Therefore a piece of dry bread is better than a good meal.

Other syllogisms are:

> If X is A (antecedent) then it is B (consequent)
> X is A (or X is not B)
> Therefore X is B (or X is not A)

Note that it does not work the other way round. You cannot get an irrefutable conclusion from either 'X is not A', nor from 'X is B'. As is often the case, one can see this from a simple example:

> If Mary is Peter's sister then she lives in Bristol
> Mary is Peter's sister (Mary does not live in Bristol)
> Therefore Mary lives in Bristol (Mary is not Peter's sister)

but one cannot deduce anything about where Mary lives from the fact that she is not Peter's sister, nor deduce anything about her relationship with Peter from the fact that she lives in Bristol. Think about it!

The first syllogism we looked at is called a 'categorical' one. The syllogism we have just explored was a 'hypothetical' one. The next syllogism is a 'disjunctive' one.

> X is either A or B
> X is A
> Therefore X cannot be B

> Margaret is either good or bad
> She is good
> Therefore she cannot be bad

You can begin to see the problems in even apparently simple logical arguments and they basically relate to the definition of words. It is for this reason that Socratic questioning as a means of teaching is so powerful. It forces the student to look at the meaning of words and what is being said. It clarifies the situation and its meaning.

Logical deductions can be classified in other ways in terms of relationships. Thus:

Transitive relations: If A has a property related to B, and B has it to C, then A has it to C. Eg, 'ancestor of', 'included in'.

Intransitive relations: If A has it to B, and B to C, then A cannot have it to C. Eg, 'half of', '10% larger than'.

Non-transitive relations: If A has it to B, and B to C, then A may or may not have it to C. Eg, 'friend of'.

Symmetrical: A is the same as B, B is the same as A. Eg, 'equal to'.

Asymmetrical: B cannot have the same relationship to A as A has to B. Eg, 'mother of'.

Non-symmetrical: B may or may not have the same relationship to A that A has to B. Eg, 'likes'.

Meaning

Words are the building blocks from which communication is constructed. The power of the spoken word is partly derived from the fact that it is easier to clarify something in face-to-face discussion than on the printed page. The use of logic in an argument is one way of clarifying the situation, but the meaning of the words used will always lie at the root of communication. It is helpful therefore to consider the meaning of words as an essential part of the argument and reasoning process. Students should be challenged on their use of words and urged to ask for, and expect, clarity of meaning when listening to others or taking part in discussion.

There is an imperative need to define ambiguous words or one will end up by talking at cross-purposes. This can often be the cause of disagreement over descriptive statistics. What, for example, does one mean by a 'criminal', or 'criminal behaviour'? Does this refer to those who have been caught and punished? What of those who are not caught? And what 'crimes' are to be counted? Those that are reported, or those that happen but are not always reported? Does the crime rate depend on whether certain behaviour is regarded as criminal? And what about the age of the perpetrator – are children to be regarded as criminals?

Above all, it is important to realize that words are only symbols which stand for things in the outside world. The relationship between words and the things they represent is purely arbitrary. If the meanings of the words 'sun' and 'moon' were interchanged then the sun would shine at night. Words do not possess any magical power; the power they have derives from the situation in which they are used. The use of swear words (in the sense of vulgarities or blasphemies) depends on the social expectations of the audience. (It is interesting that the use of swear words in the sense of avowing also depends on the social or legal environment.) However, although words do not have magical powers in the literal sense, they can appear to bestow good or bad qualities on the things that they name. For example 'peace', 'Christian', 'community' are generally regarded as having an aura of goodness, while 'vagrant', 'lecher', 'dirt', 'slime' have an aura of badness or evil. The clarity of an argument can be easily clouded by the use of such emotionally toned words and the skilled arguer will spot them and substitute a non-emotional equivalent where possible or will at least point out that they do not automatically bestow this quality on other things.

It is worth noticing that ambiguity can extend to things other than individual words. It is possible to have ambiguous sentences – a fact made much use of in fortune telling, and by none other than the Oracle at Delphi which gave out such predictions as 'The Greeks the Persians shall subdue'. Even a two-word utterance such as 'Time flies' can be taken as an instruction to measure the flying speed of insects. In speech this opportunity for ambiguity is greatly extended because of the ability to introduce tonal variations of emphasis. The speaker says, 'Nothing is too good for her.' Depending on the emphasis, or the amount of irony in the voice, this may be taken as adulation or disdain. Finally, ambiguity can extend to the state of affairs where the impact of a statement depends on its contextual significance. The statement, 'John did not beat his wife this week', can carry a great deal of meaning in some circumstances, and be virtually meaningless in others.

It is obviously important, then, to ask for and give definitions of terms. This does not mean that one is free to define terms in any way one pleases. It is only Humpty Dumpty who can say, 'When I use a word it means what I want it to mean.' Unfortunately there are words which everyone wants to commandeer for his or her own, such words as 'democracy', 'freedom', 'liberty', which are redefined to suit the occasion and the speaker. Thus one has 'freedom from unemployment', 'free speech', 'total freedom', 'freedom from want', which sound magnificent but on closer inspection are not always defined sufficiently well to form the basis of rational argument.

The question, though, is how one can define the meaning of something. It is helpful when faced with pedantic arguers to realize that there can be different ways in which something can be defined. There are three general methods of defining. First, by description, a synonym. We can say that 'will' is the same as 'volition', 'determination', or 'intention'. But this can be a circular process if the listener is not familiar with the synonyms; in any case it misses out the subtle differences between similar words. Then there is the use of examples. This is sometimes the only, or at least the most effective, way to define something, particularly when referring to concepts such as 'love', 'sound', 'picture', 'colour'.

The third method is that of analysis, ie differentiating within a particular class of concepts or items. If the argument is about equal opportunities, for example, and the particular subject is that of interviewing, then it is useful to define it in terms of, say, selection interviewing as distinct from disciplinary or appraisal or some other type of interview. The best analytical definitions are convertible, that is to say there is a complete equivalence between the definition and the word. The form is that, 'All X are Y and only X are Y'; otherwise the definition becomes either too broad or too narrow. If we take the question of defining what we mean by 'democratic', for example, we would presumably use a definition that was wide enough to include all systems whereby people had the right to have a secret ballot for representatives, and certain freedoms to express opinions. We could then say that every system that exhibited those characteristics was a democratic one, and that only those systems were democratic. If we insisted that democracy literally meant that everyone voted on everything then this would exclude almost every practical system of government or management; if we said that it meant that 'the power rested with the people', then we would find that the definition was so wide and general that every government would claim to be democratic in its own way.

A good analytical definition must be capable of being checked against the actual situation to determine whether the definition holds. It is clear that some things such as 'colour' or 'happiness' are going to be difficult to define in this way. Sometimes indeed such a definition can be misleading. To define 'health' as 'the absence of illness' ignores the idea of health being a positive state rather than a negative one. The definition has used one state or condition to define another instead of starting from scratch to identify those aspects of a living organism which one calls healthy.

Methods of argument

Any argument must be logical but, quite apart from the formal logic of a debate, the student needs to learn the techniques by which one can show the truth of a statement or the relevance of the evidence. Argument has its own methods and procedures whereby the speaker and listener can follow a common pattern of thought more easily.

It is always useful when looking at methods and procedures to see whether there are any frameworks already devised to categorize the material one is looking at. Fortunately there are two great historical sources we can look at in relation to methods of argument: the system used by Socrates and the system used in the Babylonian Talmud, or Jewish code of conduct. They are very similar in many ways and the following list is an amalgamation of both. There is a formal traditional pattern to the classical argument; a questioner, called in the Talmud the 'makshan', and a replier, called the 'tartzan'.

From authority: 'As Margaret Smith says . . .' 'The Pope said in his speech the other day . . .'

There is no doubt that being able to quote an authoritative source is a powerful aid in any argument. If Professor X has said that something is so, then there is a natural disposition to believe it must be so. This may be all very well when Professor X happens to be an expert on that particular subject; unfortunately there is a tendency to pay high regard to figures of authority such as professors, company directors, members of the government, senior officers in the services, or priests and bank managers, irrespective of what they are discussing. This is even more noticeable when it comes to the opinions of pop stars and film stars.

By comparison or analogy: 'After all, using a conciliation service or arbitration is like having a referee at a football match.'

This is a common form of argument. It is used where something can be deduced from accepted teaching which it closely resembles. The problem, however, is that comparison only means being similar to something, not identical in all respects. The danger of using analogies is that they may be used in the sense of 'the same as' when all that can be claimed is that they are 'very like' the object being discussed. Hence it is possible to refute a comparison or analogy by differentiation as indicated next.

By differentiation: 'But you can't compare the social effects of smoking with drinking because the effects of smoking tend to affect mainly the individual whereas drinking and driving may have a fatal effect on other people.'

That is to say that one seeks to show those areas in which the two cases are different. Thus in the case of the comparison with a referee it could be pointed out that the referee has a number of very clearly defined rules to work to, and that his or her decision is binding. There is a considerable difference in the time-scale allowed for decision and, unlike the arbitrator, the referee cannot ask for more information before making that decision.

Either/or: 'If you continue on front-line duty you must be crazy; but if you ask to be taken off front-line duty because you're going crazy it shows that you can't be crazy – that's Catch 22. Whichever way you look at it, you have to continue' (Joseph Heller, *Catch 22*).

A powerful way to forestall opposition is to show that the same consequences follow irrespective of which line of argument is followed. In arguments about fox-hunting, for example, those in favour of the sport will argue that it is justified because it is a way of keeping down vermin which cost the farmer in terms of lost poultry. One could argue that either the amount of damage caused by foxes was small in comparison to the cost of mounting a hunt and therefore did not justify the suffering caused, or that if the damage was substantial then it was important to use as efficient a method of controlling foxes as possible, and that hunting was relatively inefficient. In either case the effect is to reject fox hunting as a viable activity.

On the contrary: 'You say that inflation would increase our financial problems because of the increase in interest charges on the money we borrowed, but in fact what we have built will increase in value at a greater rate, so we shall benefit in the long run.'

In some arguments it is simply a case of pointing out that it is more plausible the other way round. The proponents of psychoanalytic theory argue that people often shout or bully because they have an inferiority complex. It is, on the face of it, more plausible to argue that those who shout, bully and try to dominate are more likely to do it because they feel that they are superior to those they are intimidating. Thus it is up to the proponents of the theory to show why the more plausible cause is not acceptable.

Acceptance in part: 'Yes . . . but . . .' 'There must be limitations on freedom of expression if it hurts or offends others . . .' 'There must be a balance between power and responsibility . . .'

One of the routes to achieving compromise solutions is to identify which part of the argument is acceptable even when the whole is not. It may be argued that children must be allowed to express themselves freely or that workers should have control over their environmental working conditions. The aim is to define the areas where agreement can be obtained, and hence to highlight the areas which remain controversial.

Based on the opponent's position: 'Even if I accept that God does exist, you still have to explain how He can allow so much suffering in the world . . .' 'Even according to your own reasoning there must still be some occasions when the wind strength rises above 60 miles per hour and therefore the bridge structure . . .'

Sometimes it is not worth challenging the other side's initial proposition if one can reach the same result by accepting their statement for the sake of argument and showing that it still leads to the same results. One can accept that farming animals may be morally justified but still argue that a vegetarian diet is more healthy.

Expose flaws in the logic: 'All cats are four-legged animals; Snoopy is a four-legged animal; it doesn't follow that therefore Snoopy is a cat.'

There are a number of common fallacies in the logic which people use in argument; these are dealt with in detail in the next section of this chapter.

Defining conditions: 'But that only holds because you are assuming the conditions that hold in Western Europe . . .' 'Don't forget that ten years ago we would not have been so familiar with computers . . .'

Changing the geographical, political, social or historical perspective will often change the argument. Arguments about fishing rights make the implicit assumption that there are other forms of food available. If one is considering the position of the Eskimo (Inuit) then this assumption is no longer valid.

States of mind: 'People will usually call the police . . .' 'You'd have expected her to turn the valve off . . .'

Some parts of an argument are almost bound to depend on assumptions about human behaviour. In practice these assumptions are socially and culturally determined and should be questioned if necessary. You would not expect English and Americans to behave in the same way when sitting opposite strangers in a train.

Readmission of previously rejected argument: 'In reality we have to accept the offer . . .' 'It would be better to do something about it than be obstinate . . .'

Depending on the circumstances and purpose of the argument, it may be better to arrive at a compromise solution by accepting part of the opposition's argument and looking for the best solution available, rather than to founder in a sterile theoretical argument. This is particularly so when the argument is part of a negotiation. It may be impossible to prove a causal link between smoking and cancer, pornography and violence, pin-up advertisements and the lack of opportunities for women, but in practice it may be useful to assume at least a partial connection.

Questioning the obvious: 'It may seem obvious, but why do men have to wear a suit and tie to an interview?' 'Is frequent washing necessarily healthy?' 'Are women less likely to commit crimes of violence – particularly against children?'

One of the most pernicious traps that a timid or insecure person can fall into is being afraid to question what may appear at first sight to be obvious. All too often things are assumed which beg the question. Within the constraints of the time available, everything should be open to questioning.

Resolving contradictions between sources: 'Both parties claim to be concerned to raise the living standards of the poor; but one side assumes that the way to do it is by redistribution of the available resources, the other by increasing the total resources available.'

Very often apparent contradictions turn on the different meanings

111

which opposing groups attach to particular words, or assumptions on the methods which will be used to achieve particular aims. It may appear to be a contradiction for the Mother's Union to limit membership to married women, or for two Christian sects to fight each other, or for two expert witnesses to disagree with one another in court. The resolution of these apparent contradictions often reveals the basic assumptions which lie behind people's beliefs.

Limitations of scope: 'When it says that "to him that hath shall be given" it really refers to a distinction between those who are willing to contribute to, and work for the community, and those who sit and do nothing . . .' 'When you argue against a police force carrying guns, you must be referring to those countries where the citizen is not allowed to carry firearms . . .'

Sweeping generalizations, particularly when backed up by some authority, are difficult to argue against unless one can spot that the generalizations are in fact only applicable to a limited set of conditions. Even the argument that everyone likes to be happy (to be free . . .) must have some boundaries, such as the fact that their happiness (freedom . . .) does not interfere with the happiness of others.

Reductio ad absurdum: 'If you follow your argument to its logical conclusion . . .' 'If safety were a prime consideration we would never get out of bed . . .'

It is worth looking at the consequences of following an argument to its logical conclusion if only to enable those involved to clarify the boundaries of their dispute. If, for example, we insisted on high standards of proof for everything, it would be very difficult to carry on with normal life, as we could never be sure of anything without going back to first principles or seeing it with our own eyes. What evidence is there that anyone has actually gone into space? Pictures, statements . . . but what concrete evidence does the individual citizen have?

In the classic Talmudic argument the components of argument that have been listed above are presented with a limited vocabulary of these technical terms. They are cryptic and do not always spell out the meaning, it being assumed that the listener or reader will fill in the meaning from a knowledge of the terms used. There is no particular striving for rhyme, rhythm, alliteration, or any of the other techniques of oratory used to persuade. The persuasion comes from the force of the argument itself, together with the construction of the argument to build up to a climax which is designed to clinch the matter.

Fallacies

The number of fallacies in argument are legion. Much of the time in argument is spent in identifying the errors or loopholes in the other person's statements and then proceeding to put forward one's next point as a counter move. A knowledge of the common fallacies is therefore an essential step towards being able to hold one's own in a discussion. It is something which can best be taught by examples taken from discussion as and when they occur, but a preliminary discussion of the main areas will alert students to the problem. The range of fallacies has been arbitrarily grouped under five headings: Logic, Words, Distortion, Diversion and Simplification, and Error.

Logic. Perhaps the most common type of logical error is where there is an implied choice between two answers, whereas in reality there are other possibilities available. 'Is it black or white?' This is a *false dichotomy*, known technically as the fallacy of *the excluded middle*. Clearly not everything has to be either black or white; there are shades of grey in between. This fallacy shows itself in such arguments as: 'She is either sane or insane'; 'it is either good or bad'. More dangerous, and less obvious are the arguments: 'Every sector of society is either proletarian or capitalist'; 'you are either with us or against us.'

A different type of fallacy is where two propositions are linked by a common element and the assumption is made that this sharing of the common element somehow brings them together. 'Cats climb trees, squirrels climb trees, therefore cats must basically be squirrels.' This is known as the fallacy of the *undistributed middle*, which unfortunately makes it easy to confuse with the previous one. The description, however, refers to the element which is shared; the concept of 'distribution' is that it says something about all the members of the class to which it refers. In this case the middle term is 'climb', and the erroneous assumption is that all tree climbers must be the same. A practical example of this fallacy would be: 'Teachers in school X agree with the use of corporal punishment, fascists agree with the use of corporal punishment, therefore the teachers in school X are fascists.'

There are of course the straightforward misuses of the simple syllogism:

> All Xs are Y,
> Z is an X,
> Therefore Z is a Y.

113

While this is true, the modified version is not (All Xs are Y, Z is a Y, therefore Z is an X) because although all Xs are Y, not all Ys are X. Hence the fallacy: 'All cats are four-legged animals, Snoopy is a four-legged animal, therefore Snoopy is a cat.' The points to watch out for are, for example, that 'all' or 'every' is implied ('The Japanese believe that . . .'), that the meaning of the terms do not change between premise and conclusion ('There are few reasons to support the idea, but we have a few reasons we would like to put forward to support it'; 'He gets home at 5.30, but he really does not feel at home there') and that conclusions are not drawn from two negative premises ('Acupuncture, herbal remedies, homeopathic medicine, aromatherapy, psychotherapy, etc, do not use drugs, therefore they are all similar').

A further fallacy which has already been mentioned is the confusion of *correlation and causation*. Someone once discovered that over a period of years there was a correlation between the number of storks migrating from Sweden, and the number of babies born in Britain but no one would suggest that one was the cause of the other. It is also true that the IQ score of children in any given grade will be correlated with their shoe size. The reason is that each grade contains children whose age can vary by as much as one year; the shoe size is a measure of age, not the cause or result of intelligence. This fallacy is a ubiquitous one since many arguments hinge on the idea that because two things are connected, one must be the cause of the other ('Firms with the most profits and productivity tend to spend more on training . . .').

The last fallacy in this section is one which goes like this: 'One hair does not make a beard, two hairs do not either. At what stage can you say that the addition of one hair makes it a beard?' This is the *denial of incremental change*. It is a difficult one to deal with until one realizes that logically it would deny the difference between black and white, and that it is really a question of definition. The point is that one is being asked to make a definition on artificial grounds. Sometimes, as in the law, or with scientific standards, it is necessary to have absolute dividing lines; in normal usage it is not a helpful way of working.

Words

The idea that all words are by their very nature closely defined leads to a great number of misunderstandings in argument. There have been schools of philosophy which argued that words and things were somehow inextricably associated with one another and this has given us a false idea of the quality of words. A word is only a convenient form of communication for an idea. The word should reflect whatever the user wishes to communicate. The argument as to whether rhubarb is a vegetable or a fruit is not an argument about facts but an argument about the use of words. This is the fallacy of *confusing words with facts*.

This is very similar to another fallacy, that of *begging the question, or tautology, or circular argument*. A typical case would be where someone is arguing that some Christians are not very good at keeping the moral codes, that for example she had seen a number of people come out of church, drink heavily in a local bar, and then drive off in their car in an erratic manner. The response might be, 'Ah well, those people aren't really Christian', ie the respondent's definition of 'Christian' is such as automatically to exclude badly behaved people.

Another example might be that of hedonism, ie where someone is arguing that people only do things for their own pleasure. If it is pointed out that there are many examples of altruism, ranging from people giving away all their money, to people putting themselves in extreme danger of life and limb in order to help others, then the original proposer is likely to reply that they must enjoy doing these things, otherwise they wouldn't do them! Thus in both cases the speaker is assuming what in fact they should be seeking to prove.

A further instance where language plays an important part is in *generalizations*. There are two separate but related issues here. The first one is the *implying of 'all'* when only 'some' is justified. The typical statement is that 'women are shorter than men', 'skinheads are untrustworthy', 'members of an enemy country are evil', 'capital punishment has/has not proved an effective deterrent in other countries'. This fallacy overlaps with that of *proof by selected instances*, an obvious but commonly used ploy.

The other manifestation of the problem of generalization is that of *stereotyping*. This is so common as to need hardly any comment. Everyone must be familiar with the stereotyped assumptions which accompany the words 'woman', 'man', 'Jew', 'engineer', 'politician', 'car salesman', 'professor', 'bank manager', and so on. The main thing is to ensure that their assumption in an argument is immediately challenged.

Finally, words by their very nature are ambiguous, which leads easily to the process of *equivocation*, particularly in the English language. We have already seen an example of this at work in the use of the word 'nothing' in the sentence 'nothing is better than . . .', it is even more

115

striking when the word in question is that of a country or nation. Consider the following: 'Britain fought Germany in two world wars'; 'Britain educates every child over the age of five'; 'Britain loves fox-hunting'; 'Britain suffers from pollution due to acid rain'; 'Britain feels that she should enter the European Market'; 'Britain produces milk and whisky'; 'Britain is the home of parliamentary democracy'; Britain is covered with a network of roads and railways'.

The word 'Britain' variously means: 'those who were in the armed forces and associated administration', 'those who are responsible for the education system', 'those (possibly a minority) who approve of blood sports', either 'the land' or 'farmers' or 'the fish' who are affected by acid rain, 'members of the government', 'dairy farmers and distillers', 'a theoretical concept covering both geographical location and the government', and finally 'a physical surface which is part of the earth's crust'. And yet the word can be used in a variety of contexts and by a variety of speakers without anyone realizing that they are talking about different entities.

Distortion

Arguments can very easily become heated. In those circumstances you can all too readily succumb to the temptation of *extending your propositions* further than you had intended in order to make your point more forcibly. You may start out with a specific proposition relating to killing certain types of animal for their skins, shall we say. Before you know where you are you find yourself attacking (or defending) the killing of animals for food, for research, as vermin, etc. Or an argument about the application of sanctions in South Africa is extended to the application of sanctions against a whole list of countries for a variety of reasons. The secret is to be clear as to where your boundaries are and to refuse to extend them. This is often the problem with debates on such sensitive issues as euthanasia, or abortion. Very often one side in the argument will want to encompass a much larger issue than the original one. This is not to say that many of these issues relate to much deeper and more fundamental ones; the choice of how deep to pursue them must, however, lie with each protagonist.

The use of analogies is common in discussion and explanation, it can lead to erroneous conclusions when a *false analogy* is used, or when the analogy is pushed too far. It may be all right to compare the 'pressure' which the instincts exert to that exerted by steam in a pressure vessel,

116

and to argue that this energy can be usefully diverted into various tasks and projects, but to introduce other properties of steam, such as its high temperature, or its capacity to condense into water may be imaginative, but not helpful to a logical argument. Similarly the attempt to compare the complex economy of the country with the running of a grocer's shop is over-simplistic and liable to run into major difficulties. The Victorian idea that Virtue would grow by being watered by tears and blood ignored the fact that one could equally well argue that Vice might grow when watered in the same fashion, and that manure anyway was also part of the process!

Embedded assumptions are particularly difficult to spot when they come as part of a question. The question, 'How do you account for poltergeists then?' is a challenge to the debater until one realizes that it assumes the existence of poltergeists, which may be something which should not be taken for granted. Indeed the question of their existence may be fundamental to the whole argument. Another frequently used technique is to argue that one's position is the *mean between two extremes*. It is human nature to play safe by plumping for the middle path, but almost every view can be seen as the mean between two extremes. The small, compact car is midway between a bicycle and a family car, which in turn is midway between the compact car and a luxury limousine, which is itself midway between a family car and a private plane . . . Smoking a pipe can be seen as midway between non-smoking and smoking cigarettes, smoking cigarettes is midway between non-smoking and taking drugs. Having a specially selected group of armed police is half-way between a completely unarmed police force and a fully armed one, but a fully armed police force is itself mid-way between a completely unarmed one and control by the military.

Diversion and over-simplification

The commonest form of diversion is the *non-sequitur* which can arise from casual asides such as 'just like a man' or 'just like a woman'. The argument that something is acceptable because there is an even greater evil to fight falls into this category as well. One must avoid being side-tracked in this way. The other type of diversion is to try to diminish the other person's argument not by logic, but by impugning his or her motives. This process of attacking the person rather than the argument is called *arguing ad hominem*. The fact that someone may well be prejudiced or biased does not indicate whether or not their argument is sound. It is reasonable to expect that many of those who advocate socialism are partly motivated by an envy of the rich, many of those who espouse capitalism or conservatism must want to hold on to their wealth. The question as to which system is the better one, however, should be argued independently of these personal motives.

Statements about the personal qualities of the other person rather than the facts and logic of the argument are only acceptable if the integrity or expertise of the person is relevant to the subject of the argument.

Over-simplification is much easier to spot although not always easy to counter. It often shows itself in the use of slogan-type phrases: 'Men are descended from monkeys', 'Eating fish gives you brains', 'Eating carrots makes you see in the dark', 'You can tell they're untrustworthy by their eyes', 'The Swedes are a mournful race', 'The Italians are very excitable', 'What's good for business is good for the country', 'Woman's place is in the home'. Not only does simplification show itself by the style of telling; the use of sayings itself can lead to illogical argument. There are many well-known sayings which can be misinterpreted or misused; 'The exception proves (ie tests) the rule', 'There's no smoke without fire'. The unreliability of using them as a part of an argument can be quickly seen if pairs of sayings are considered: 'Look before you leap' but 'He who hesitates is lost', 'Too many cooks spoil the broth', but 'The more the merrier', 'If a thing's worth doing it's worth doing well', but 'Half a loaf is better than no bread'.

Error

In many ways this is the simplest and most obvious of fallacies in argument and within this part of it the use of *faulty evidence* is the most clear-cut. Evidence may be faulty because it is incomplete, drawn from unreliable or uncheckable sources, misquoted, misinterpreted, or just plain wrong. Rather more subtle is the use of *false premises*, particularly when they are popularly held beliefs such as the idea that 'Gentlemen prefer blondes', that 'Blondes are more promiscuous than brunettes', or that 'Building up strong defences is the best road to peace'. These are insidious arguments because they sometimes pass in the course of discussion without being challenged.

Sometimes evidence can be faulty or incomplete; *negative evidence* presents a different problem. This relates to the unfair practice of arguing that because there is no positive evidence it somehow proves the opposite view must be correct. It is known as *argumentum ad ignorantiam*, arguing from the lack of knowledge, saying 'Well, you can't disprove it'. This falsely shifts the onus of proof on to the antagonist, whereas it should be on the proposer to prove his or her point. Another way of looking at it is to realize that it does not prove anything to say that, 'The majority of witnesses did not see the accused do it', when in fact they did not see anything at all.

Finally there is the problem of *confusing fact with inference*. Someone driving a large car is assumed to be wealthy, someone who does not contribute to a flag day must be mean, graffiti must have been carried out by a teenager, a plume of vapour over a power station shows that it must be polluting the atmosphere. The conclusions from observation must always be open to challenge and it is part of the virtue of argument that it exposes these readily accepted ideas to the cold wind of analysis and proof.

Getting the floor

By now you and your students may be sympathizing with those who burst out in the middle of an argument and accuse the participants of being too pedantic, too pernickety. The aim of reading about and studying the different aspects of argument is not to conduct argument in a highly formal and detailed way, but to be able to spot the fallacies and errors when your instincts tell you that you have been sidestepped. It is useful to be able to identify the particular logical falsehood or slip so as to develop more easily the counter argument or refutation. Reading about the subject encourages an awareness of the range of stratagems available and the ploys you may meet.

In reality a normally conducted argument will skip many of the logical steps discussed above. The listener brings much knowledge and experience to bear to fill in the gaps and this enables one to short-circuit a lot of laborious explanation. Consider, 'He'd like to be chairman, but he hasn't much experience', or 'When Mary heard the ice-cream van, she remembered her birthday money and ran into the house'. The reader has no difficulty in filling in all the assumptions which connect the post of chairman with experience, or in recognizing that Mary is a child and the house is her home. This phenomenon is known as an *enthymeme* and occurs when there is a logical rhetorical syllogism in which some elements are deliberately missed out. It enables us to conduct our discussions on the basis of an assumed shared culture which supplies the missing sections. This is what makes the difference between a flowing, stimulating discussion and a pedantic, stilted one. Nevertheless one must not allow assumptions to remain if there are legitimate grounds for challenging them.

Having studied the methods of argument, its logic and fallacies, we may now feel ready to go out and persuade others of our ideas and fill them with an enthusiasm for following our lead. In the practical world, however, logic and clear argument are not enough; one has to use methods that appeal to the emotions and can sway an audience. This is the realm of rhetoric and persuasion; it is the subject of the next chapter.

In rhetoric one uses such devices as anecdotes and metaphors because lack of time forces the speaker to use vivid and instantly assimilable examples. Furthermore the use of emotion fixes the ideas more strongly and ensures that they are not forgotten. On the other hand, emotion must be used with caution and there are guidelines to be followed when using fear as a motivator for example.

However skilled and articulate the person, however logical and clear the argument, all will be to no avail if he or she is unable to get a word in edgeways. In our culture conversation consists of one person speaking at a time and normally there are no silences in between the utterances. Pauses tend to get filled. If there are no formal rules and no control over who is speaking (as there might be in debate, committee or debriefing) it is vital to understand the way in which one speaker unconsciously signals the end of his or her contribution, and how others signal their desire to speak. It is also necessary to understand how people 'hold the floor' by techniques which enable them to avoid interruption. By understanding this it is possible either to ensure that you get a fair hearing, or alternatively to prevent others from hogging the floor to the exclusion of those who have not had a chance to speak.

These are some of the matters considered in the next chapter, which looks at the practical ways in which the art of rhetoric helps people put their ideas across and the ways in which students may learn to express themselves and their ideas more effectively.

7. Presentation and persuasion

Origins of oratory and rhetoric

The human voice has the power to affect and stimulate the emotions in a way which the written word cannot. This, quite apart from the fact that in a pre-literate age the audience for written material was limited, was largely the reason why such an emphasis was placed on the training of young men from the Greek and Roman aristocracy in the arts and skills of oratory and rhetoric. It was regarded as character-forming, and as a part of the study of language, but it was also of inestimable value as a practical skill in the public arena of the Roman forum or Greek agora where speakers were questioned and challenged to argue their case. It is a custom which has come down to us in the form of the hustings, Speakers' Corner (in London's Hyde Park), the whistle stop, or the chautauqua lecture meetings. In a civilization where decisions were made in a democratic way, by argument and discussion in public, it was vital to be able to express oneself verbally in front of a large audience. The audiences of today may be more variable in size, but it is still important to be able to persuade and move a meeting or a group of colleagues, to change their attitudes or obtain their backing for a new enterprise. To that extent rhetoric should be part of all education and training.

Although the speaker has at his or her command the most powerful tool ever devised for influencing other human beings, namely the human voice, nevertheless the task is not as easy as it might seem at first sight. The reason for this is that the first step is to hold the attention of the audience. The normal reason for listening carefully to another person is because in a small group one has the expectation of taking one's turn in speaking; it is important therefore to listen and take note of what the speaker is saying. This is not the case in a large audience or group which is listening to a solo speaker. Nor is it customary in normal conversation or other everyday modes of speech to have such long

121

periods of speech from one person. It is very easy to get bored and to switch off; literally so in the case of television. The speaker must stimulate and entertain the audience at the same time as putting across a case.

Structure

As with any effective use of language, rhetoric has a structure and form which should be followed. It was Cicero who established the five 'offices', or steps which comprised the complete package. They were:

Invention, the initial collecting of material;
Disposition, the arrangement of the material into a suitable form;
Memory, the memorizing of the key points to avoid having to read the speech;
Elocution or Style, the fitting of the right words to the topic, the speaker, audience and occasion;
Pronunciation, the actual delivery and action.

We shall not be following this sequence exactly, but we still need to understand the necessity for preparation, for form and style, and for effective delivery so as to have the maximum impact on the audience. We shall be looking at structure, then at the audience itself. After that we look at style, at the presentation of information, and finally at the tricks of the trade used to hold the floor and attract applause. (It should be noted that the remainder of this chapter uses the public speech as a convenient model to discuss, but the issues and techniques are in essence the same for one person trying to persuade another in a small group discussion or dialogue as for someone addressing a large gathering. The framework is the same; only the scale is different.)

The style of this chapter is somewhat different from that of other chapters in that it is more directly related to the individual student, though the arts of persuasion and presentation are relevant to many of the elements of a teacher's work; to that extent this chapter may also be regarded as a guide for the teacher. Presentation skills are, like other practical skills such as walking, cycling, craftwork, and sport, essentially something which needs practice and practical experience. The most important role of the tutor, therefore, is to provide the opportunity to get this experience and to use the material given here to suggest ways of improving performance. The chapter may therefore also be regarded as the basis of a text for the student although mediated by the teacher. Hence it will be found to use a more direct and personal style which is felt to be more appropriate to the message. After all, one of the prime considerations in presentation is to match the style of delivery to the intended audience!

The framework of a presentation is much the same as any other communication. There is an introduction, a development and a conclusion. In the introduction it is useful to describe the structure of the rest of the speech and to put it into a context either in terms of the time, the place, the topic, or the logic of cause and effect. This is the time to show how the material connects with other things that have gone before.

The development should only try to cover three or four main items; audiences cannot absorb more than this because the dynamic and active quality of sound is also the very thing that makes it difficult to recall afterwards. A small number of main points well made are worth far more than a rambling discourse which no one can remember. And at the end there must be a considered attempt to give the audience something to take away with them; a summary, a proposal, a call for support or a vote of thanks. At all events this part of the presentation must not be rushed, and must have a clear purpose behind it.

Persuasion

Persuasion is the art of modifying the attitudes of others in an intended direction and its success must therefore be evaluated in relation to where the recipient of the message stood to begin with. The term 'modification' does not necessarily imply change, in some cases people may be persuaded to stand firm against the forces of change.

There are two mediating factors which come into play. The listener must first of all receive the message and then yield to it. These factors tend to work in opposite directions, so that, for example, an anxious person may be easy to change, but not very receptive to messages in the first instance. Similarly a self-confident or very intelligent person may be well able to receive the message but not easily persuaded to change. It is necessary to ensure that both factors are taken into consideration.

Anyone interested in the skills of persuasion would do well to study the advertisements on television. Many of them have common underlying structures. First they have to get the viewers attention, then build up confidence, then stimulate desire, and finally instil a sense of urgency and a response. We shall be looking at some of these aspects later in this chapter; at this point we will look briefly at the question of stimulating desire. There is a useful matrix which describes the situation:

Keep the 'good'	Get rid of the 'bad'
PROTECTION	RELIEF
Get a 'good'	Avoid a 'bad'
ACQUISITION	PREVENTION

It is a matter of judgment as to what motivates a particular person or group of people, but it is likely to fall into one of these four categories. Clearly there will be one approach if the audience is worried or concerned to avoid or get rid of something and another approach in the contrasting situation where they basically expect to gain something. In particular this raises the question of the effectiveness of fear as a means of persuasion. Many campaigns in the health field, starting with the fight against dental decay and more recently with the publicity about Aids, have relied on creating an atmosphere of fear to get across their message. It is easy to see that fear may be over-used and boomerang back by either creating a feeling that the speaker is exaggerating, or by inducing a resistance in the listener, causing them to shut their mind to the message. Fear appeals most effectively when the following conditions are met:

1. The source of the information is highly creditable;
2. The information is absolutely specific;
3. The solution is easily implemented;
4. The unfavourable event is highly likely to occur and the listener understands this.

The two basic ways of changing behaviour are what are known as 'classical' conditioning and 'operant' or 'instrumental' conditioning. In the case of classical conditioning you pair or connect the required attitude or behaviour with a desirable image or quality. This is what is happening when a well-known sports personality sponsors a particular product or when we associate a proposal with things or words that are accepted as being 'good', like 'peace', 'motherhood', 'protecting the environment'. The mechanism of operant conditioning is to reward correct responses. This is what happens when an audience applauds, because in the process of applauding they are also giving themselves an enjoyable activity as a break from listening. In a more direct sense it is the basis of award-giving ceremonies, both large pre-planned ones and spontaneous praise or recognition.

Another psychological factor is what is known as 'cognitive dissonance'. People unconsciously try to diminish any contradiction between what they do or say and what they believe. The curious thing is that they are just as likely to change their beliefs to fit in with what they say or do as to change their actions to suit their beliefs. Indeed one psychologist has suggested that we actually use our own behaviour, reactions and statements to discover our attitudes. It is a case of 'If that's what I said, or did, then I must believe X'. An important method of persuasion is therefore to encourage the person to do or say things publicly that fall in line with the attitude you want to install. Afterwards the person will tend to adjust his or her beliefs in order to reduce the discrepancy between action or statements and beliefs. There is a balance to be achieved. The individual must be pressured enough to comply with the ideas or proposals, but not put under so much pressure that he or she feels there is no choice. This is why legislation can be effective in changing attitudes provided that it is not too extreme or punitive, and also why it can be effective to put someone in a position where they have to defend the 'official' position.

The sequence of events which is normally followed in any planned persuasion is as follows. First, establish that there is a need which is not being satisfactorily met. Next, establish that there is a real urgency to meet the need. After that, offer a clear solution and show how to overcome objections. Last, ask for specific help and commitment towards the solution.

There is a danger that the orator gets so carried away with his or her message that a patronizing attitude to the listener is taken. This is fatal. It is essential that the listener is regarded as a partner and not talked down to. Moreover there is a tendency among inexperienced speakers to describe new or complex ideas from their own personal point of view and to use examples and pictures which are meaningful to them. More experienced speakers consciously put themselves in the listener's place. But in order to do this one has to target the message for the particular audience and this implies an understanding of each individual audience and its characteristics.

The audience

It may seem an obvious point, but the audience should be the most important part of any speaker's consideration. The plain fact is that many speakers are more concerned with their own interests than those of the audience. It is essential to consider the audience in detail before planning a speech or presentation.

One way to anticipate the needs and attitudes of the audience is to ask someone who has already spoken to them, or failing that, to use your general knowledge of their group or class. Analyse them by factors or parameters such as : age, sex, economic status, occupation, parents' occupation, education, intelligence, group affiliations, geographical area, nationality/race, religion, class, and hobbies. This may seem a daunting list, but many of these parameters will already be unconsciously taken into account, and it is useful as a check-list to ensure that you do not overlook something which could lead you to offend or irritate someone. A knowledge of the audience will help you to select the most appropriate and relevant examples.

There are some key questions to ask yourself about an audience:

1. Do the members of the audience consider the subject non-controversial? If so, you are safe in presenting 'facts'. If not, however, then beware, because one 'fact' which is disputed may throw in doubt your whole argument; the audience may interpret all your information as being biased and arguable.
2. How deeply are they committed? A failure to oppose/support their ideas actively may be interpreted as bias on the opposite side, not just as an attempt to be objective. Similarly an attempt to be objective without first disclosing what the audience already knows is the self-interest of the speaker will be liable to be misinterpreted.
3. Do the members of the audience accept the speaker as the authority? If not, the point about bias made in the previous paragraph will apply. On the other hand, if they do regard the speaker as the authority then it is amazing how much they will accept. The phenomenon of 'glossolalia', or speaking in tongues (as demonstrated today in various Pentecostal denominations), shows that listeners can have faith in speakers no matter how incoherent (in the literal sense) their utterances may be.

Other types of audience:

1. Hostile audiences who disagree with you
   (a) Establish rapport. Identify with them in some area common to you both.
   (b) Yes ... but. Go from areas of agreement to areas of disagreement.
   (c) Establish general principles before specific proposals.
   (d) If possible use the first occasion to establish credibility; argue on the next one.
   (e) Use credible sources of facts and information.
   (f) Use humour (but not jokes). If you do use humour it is worth noting that the joke should be against yourself, not others. If in doubt – leave it out.
   (g) Consider less attractive options first and then broach your own proposal (the method of residues).
2. Sympathetic audiences
   (a) Use extended references to the known facts.
   (b) Use colourful and imaginative language.
   (c) Dramatize rather than prove.
   (d) Ask for specific behavioural commitments.
   (e) Overstate rather than understate.
3. Uninformed, apathetic audiences
   (a) Get their attention (use the techniques described at the end of this chapter).
   (b) Decode, ie carefully explain the information.
   (c) Give a little information at a time and repeat with variations; use plenty of examples.
   (d) Appear to inform rather than persuade.
   (e) Stress your own expertise.
   (f) Give only one side of the picture (for a well-informed audience give both sides).
   (g) Use successful role models and examples.
4. Passive audience
   (a) Get a commitment to action.
   (b) Be specific about who, what, where, when and how.
   (c) Use role models, pick leaders.
   (d) Remind the audience that they have freedom of choice but do this *after* they have made their public commitment to action.

Remember that the audience are your partners. The occasion demands the presence of both you yourself and the audience; one is nothing without the other. It is desirable therefore to welcome audience participation (and indeed it is only this type of interactive communication that belongs in this book). In order to encourage the audience to intervene and contribute you should avoid losing them by using technical jargon outside their normal understanding, no matter how useful it is in other ways. The relationship with the audience must be maintained by being sensitive and tactful in correcting questioners, and not using humour to humiliate. On your own side, you should apologize if you are wrong. It is a good idea to vary the course, style and speed of delivery in order to keep the listeners alert; you yourself should listen and be silent when they are speaking, whether as a way of acknowledging their question, or as a way of obtaining attention when someone is chattering. It is wise to avoid the excessive use of 'I' and rather than use false modesty in the form of 'I humbly beg to say . . .', it is better to flatter the audience gently by references to them and their abilities.

Style and technique

It is easy to understand the need for special techniques and 'tricks of the trade' once the limitations of oral communication are understood. We have already noted in a previous chapter that the sound of speech is ephemeral; add to that the fact that people can only know what they can recall and it is clear that you have to organize things in speaking to an audience so that they will be able to recall what you have said after you have finished speaking. Classic rhetoric therefore uses pattern. The pattern may come in the form of rhythm, balance, repetition, contrasts, alliteration, or in the use of well-known themes such as the family, meals, fighting, or by using slogans, proverbs and recognized phrases.

In an oral culture thought and expression tend to be:

1. *Additive.* The Book of Genesis begins nearly every verse with 'And . . .'; it is this quality which makes the early version of the Bible so much easier to read aloud than the newer versions. Sentences are simple, short and accumulative in their meaning.
2. *Situational.* The speaker can refer to the 'here and now'. Written discourse has developed a more elaborate grammar to make up for the lack of existential surrounding contexts; spoken discourse can be much simpler, and in a sense less grammatical than the

written word. The author Damon Runyon has tried in his short stories to convey this feeling of the spoken word by writing entirely in the present tense, '. . . and so he goes to the table and he says . . .'

3. *Aggregative.* Words are grouped together rather than considered singly and nouns are broadened by accompanying epithets. The storyteller speaks of the 'brave soldier', the 'beautiful princess', the 'foul villain'. We follow this tradition in 'the glorious revolution', 'the glorious 4th of July', 'democratic freedom'.

4. *Redundant.* The word 'redundant' is used in the technical sense to mean that the language is repetitive, wordy, voluble. This is to cope with the problem of 'noise' which may mask a vital piece of information. Since listeners cannot go back to check on what they have heard it is important to repeat and elaborate on what one has said.

5. *Argumentative and combative.* There is a constant problem of keeping the listener's attention and being argumentative and combative is one way of holding it.

6. *Homeostatic, empathetic and participatory.* One of the key advantages of the spoken word is that it can be constantly adjusted to the interests of the audience, and the speaker can benefit from immediate feedback from the audience.

It is interesting to note in passing that Plato, who was well acquainted with the art of oratory, argues in *Phaedrus* and in the *Seventh Letter* that writing is inhuman and manufactured, that it destroys the ability to memorize, that it is unresponsive, and cannot explain itself or defend itself against criticism.

These requirements to make the spoken word more memorable and accessible have led to a number of rhetorical devices, or figures of speech, being developed and categorized. The following are some of the commonest ones; it is more important to be aware of their potential use than their actual names:

- Metaphor and simile
  Using the similarity between two things in a particular detail to allow the substitution of one for the other, either directly (simile), 'Thine eyes are like two stars', or indirectly (metaphor), 'He's a real tiger', 'The sea boiled', 'She blossomed'. An extended metaphor is called an allegory.

- Antithesis
  Contrasting pairs which are similar in length, content and grammatical structure: 'Ask not what your country can do for you; rather ask what you can do for your country.' The similarity and balance between the parts allows the audience to keep track of the concepts.
- Irony
  A statement which the audience knows is not really intended and where there is a noticeable discrepancy between the statement and the intent: 'We would all love to spend our time filling in these forms but . . .'
- Allusion
  An indirect reference to something which the audience is aware of: 'Let us today be "the few"', 'Do we really feel that these should be given "to him that hath"?'
- Apostrophe
  Addressing a person who is not actually present: 'We ask you, Mr President, to consider . . .', 'You would not want that, would you, Mrs Average Voter?', 'Look down on us, God.'
- Alliteration
  The recurrence of the same sound, 'slowly, silently, smoothly . . .'
- Anaphora
  The repetition of the same word or phrase to begin several successive lines: 'We shall fight on the beaches, we shall fight on the landing grounds, we shall fight in the fields and in the streets, we shall fight in the hills.'
- Apophasis
  Saying something by artfully declining to say it, 'I won't describe the injuries but . . .'

There are many other figures of speech which are collected and defined by scholars, but these will serve to give a taste of the variety of ways in which the language can be pressed into service to give the spoken word a more poetic and riveting quality.

The act of prayer, the words of the marriage service, and the language used in 'swearing in', all testify to the real power of words. This is particularly so with the spoken word because the words themselves cannot be seen or physically attached to other words and are not therefore to be regarded as merely labels. The sound of the spoken word can have the quality of an incantation.

While words by themselves have power, the combination of words into phrases adds greatly to their effect. This is where the question of syntax, or structure, comes in. On the whole, the aim should be to avoid compound, complex sentences, especially when they are expressed in the passive voice. It is better to be simple and direct. Thus it is better to say, 'If you want to have time to discuss this, keep your contributions short', rather than, 'In the eventuality, within the present situation which is time constrained, that it is felt to be desirable by those present that a sufficient length of period is to be made available for discussion, then those contributions which are made by those present will have to be curtailed in length.' Simplicity of statement of course does not necessarily mean simplicity of concept. Sometimes simple language can be used to express very complex and ambiguous ideas. There are many examples of this in the Bible, appropriately perhaps beginning with the statement 'In the beginning was the Word . . .'

If the word is a powerful tool, then so also is the image, the picture. Of course it is possible to show a real physical picture when giving a lecture or presentation, but in the sort of discourse which we are discussing here it is also possible to paint a picture with words and sometimes that can be even more effective than the physical one. It has been said that 'Eloquence is logic on fire', an image which itself demonstrates its own power. The storyteller can conjure up the sights and smells of other places in a unique way because he or she has access to the innermost consciousness of the listener. In the same way every speaker can penetrate the mind of the listener.

It has been pointed out earlier that we tend to talk in a continuous fashion and that those who appear to talk particularly fast are in fact only filling in the spaces between words and pausing less. This leads us to realize that the pause can be a very effective way of catching the attention of the listener and emphasizing a particular point. The inexperienced speaker is usually too embarrassed to hold a pause for long. This is a pity, because audiences are far more tolerant of pauses than speakers imagine. Silence gives the audience an opportunity to think, to catch up on what has been said, and to prepare itself for the next piece of information. The pause is a way of 'pointing' or emphasizing what follows. Some pauses are more startling and attention-grabbing than others.

In general, pauses which appear in certain 'natural' positions are not noticed. These natural positions are: before a conjunction, 'but, therefore . . .', before a pronoun, 'who, which, what, why . . .', or at the end of a clause or sentence. On the other hand pauses which occur in unnatural places can be quite startling: '. . . in front of me was a bright green (pause) . . . hat.' The pause can also be used judiciously by waiting for silence at the beginning of a speech and after any interruptions; it is extremely effective if you pause at the beginning of a summing up or final peroration.

Psychologists enjoy exploring aspects of language and behaviour, and they have contributed a great deal to the study of the spoken word. Much of their work is rather esoteric and cannot be directly applied to practical situations, but some of their findings are not only interesting but have an immediate practical application. One such finding is that it is important to give people reasons for doing things, even if the reasons are tautological, that is to say that the reason given for doing something is in fact the actual doing of it. This may seem complicated but an actual example will help. It was found in an experiment that when someone in a queue asked, 'May I use the copier ahead of you because I have to make some copies?' they obtained a better response than if they just asked to go first. The reason lies in the trigger word 'because'. The listeners heard a reason being given, and that was enough; they did not go so far as to question or analyse the reason. Thus it is wise wherever possible to give reasons for things.

Finally it is worth considering the position of talk in the media, television and radio. These invite a more conversational, intimate and conciliatory style of speech than the public platform. It is more acceptable to be seen on TV to be expressing oneself in an introspective rather than an extrovert fashion. The style has been labelled a more 'feminine' one, although this does not imply that only women can use it. Presentation on the media is a subject which could occupy a book in itself, but it is at least worth remembering that a low key style is far more appropriate.

Giving information

Although persuasion usually depends in part on the emotions and feeling, it is often necessary to impart information and factual material to an audience. The question of objectivity often arises in the course of doing this. This in turn rests on certain assumptions, in the first place that problems are matters of objective facts rather than how facts are classified or labelled. But the particular labels which are used will themselves rely on different metaphors or images. For example, one can talk about the question of devolution in terms of a comparison between fragmentation or coordination. On the other hand one could equally well describe it in terms of autonomy or central control. The images are different.

Another assumption is that all proposals for new policies must meet a demonstrated need. This ignores the possibility of taking action in order to improve an already good situation or to prevent a deterioration in the current situation. Lastly there is an assumption that it is better to concentrate on causes rather than symptoms or effects. But causes are often obscure and complex. In practice dealing with the effects in a cybernetic, feedback way so as to engender gradual changes in the system may turn out to be the best approach.

Giving the facts may therefore not always be as simple as it may sound. At all events it should be done in a structured fashion, and the structure should be sufficiently flexible to allow you to follow the audience's way of looking at the subject if need be. The essential thing is to be clear about the message. It is of little use saying, 'Guns don't kill people – people kill people', unless you explain what exactly the meaning of the saying is supposed to be. Similarly it is important to give explicit, clear instructions on what action to take. In President Nixon's famous 'Checkers' speech he appealed for telegrams of support, but did not say to where the telegrams should be sent, a mistake that could have been disastrous.

Giving information is more likely to require the use of notes than other types of communication. Notes should be written clearly on cards. Every opportunity should be taken to structure the notes by such devices as using coloured pens, using a graphic or structured layout, columns and underlining or drawing boxes round key items. Only one side of the card should be used, and they must be numbered in case you drop them. Quotations should be short and used sparingly; you should not refer back to what you yourself said some time ago unless you want to repeat it for clarity. If you have to read from your cards, do not talk while looking at the card. Pause to read the information and then deliver it while looking at the audience.

The effective delivery of any presentation, however, will depend on the ways in which you hold the floor, attract the attention of the audience, and fill them with an enthusiasm for your proposals. This is the subject of the final section of this chapter.

133

Holding the audience

A major barrier to effective communication with an audience is that of nerves. No listener can relax when confronted by a speaker who appears to be a bundle of nerves. Everyone who is involved with communicating with other people, whether it is through interviews, group discussions, lectures, or debates, is bound to suffer from nerves to a greater or lesser extent. It is nerves which keep the adrenalin flowing and enable you to give all of your attention and energy to the job in hand: actors and musicians admit that however experienced they are they always suffer from nerves before they perform. The problem then is not so much that of nerves, but preventing them from having a deleterious effect on one's presentation.

One of the most important things to bear in mind is that the audience does not want to be burdened with your problems. Therefore never start by apologizing, or drawing attention to your own unease. Irritating mannerisms are likely to be exacerbated by nerves and must be kept under control. There is no reason why you should not change your position and sit or stand, whichever feels most comfortable. Finally it is essential to look the audience in the eye and not to avoid looking at them; otherwise you will appear to be a rather shifty individual.

Remember to speak directly to the audience: the worst presentations are those which are read from a text. It may be necessary to memorize part of your argument, but you only need to memorize the key points. The audience will not mind if you are searching for words now and again, it gives them more of a feeling of being involved and they can empathize more with you. Ideally the speaker should appear to discover ideas and connections afresh during the presentation.

The instrument that you are using all this time is the human voice. It is an instrument which has a great range of quality in tone, timbre and articulation. You may have got so used to your own voice that you have ceased to notice it. Now is the time to check on whether you speak loudly and clearly enough; one thing no listener will forgive is the speaker who cannot be heard! Remember that a higher pitch tends to be associated with emotion, a lower one with calmness and assurance. First and last words are particularly important, so do not lower your voice at the ends of sentences or the ends of phrases. The end of your speech should be on a high note, not perhaps literally but metaphorically. Make sure that you have a suitable finishing phrase to hand; do not waste this valuable spot by entering into a lengthy thanks to the audience for listening to you, this can be done at the beginning, if at all.

The voice is the most important instrument of communication, but the whole body is capable of conveying messages to the listeners. Probably the most important parts of the body in this respect are the eyes. Humans are the only primate species with visible areas of white framing the iris; this means that even small movements of the eyes are visible from a distance. Eye contact is of great importance in face-to-face communication, even in large groups. The speaker should constantly scan the audience both to exert pressure on them to listen and to enhance the meaning of what he or she is saying. Facial expressions should match the meaning of what is being said, something which some people find easier that others because they have a greater natural range of facial expression.

The rest of the body conveys a message of attention, alertness, interest, or the converse of all these. Gestures can be used to emphasize points; sometimes it is noticeable that politicians beat rhythmically in the air to emphasize what they are saying, perhaps indeed a shade too obviously. The speaker who is not reading from a script will have his or her hands free to use more effectively and to coordinate both hand and body movements. Perhaps it is worth sounding a word of caution here to point out that gestures are subject to the same wide range of 'vocabulary' as the written language and that different cultures use different gestures to denote the same thing. More dangerously of course, different cultures interpret the same gesture as meaning different things. Be careful that you know and understand the conventions of your audience.

Before worrying about holding an audience, of course, it is necessary to get an opportunity to speak. In a formal setting there is no problem, but in the general discussion situation it is noticeable how some participants, usually men, are much more skilled at getting the floor and holding on to it. It is largely a matter of being sensitive to the signals which tell you that someone is getting to the end of their contribution, and of signalling your own wish to speak. End signals are the slowing down of syllables within multi-syllable words, increased gaps between words, exaggerated changes of pitch, body relaxation and the use of terms like 'finally', 'to sum up', or 'this shows . . .' Individuals have their own almost infallible signals; the British Prime Minister Margaret Thatcher, for example, almost always puts her head down, closes her mouth firmly, and clears her throat at the end of her contribution. In order to signal the wish to speak people tend to tense their body, make a sharp intake of breath, and catch the speaker's eye. Once they have the floor they are able to hold on between sections of their contribution by signalling that they have more than one thing to say, using phrases such as 'firstly . . .', or 'to begin with . . .' They are also prone to use connectors such as 'so . . .', 'but . . .', 'because . . .', 'moreover . . .', or even 'er . . . um . . .'

In a large group it is difficult for the listeners to respond verbally to the speaker as individuals. This is why audiences like to applaud (or sometimes to boo) at key points in the speaker's presentation. This acts as a relief valve for the pressure which builds up after a period of concentration and acts as an incentive to pay attention so as to know when to react. The audience likes to act in unison, but it takes very little to interfere with its ability to do so. In football crowds rhythmical singing or chanting helps to keep everyone together. The use of extended vowel sounds such as 'Hooooraaaay, boooooo . . .' make it easy to join in late. Similarly with hand clapping which also has the advantage that it is easier to sustain for a long period than loud vocalization.

The skilled speaker works on this tendency and enables the audience to show its support by providing the right cues for applause. Readers may be surprised to know how simple it is to encourage applause by means of what used to be known as a 'claptrap'. Unfortunately this word has lost its original meaning and now has a denigratory implication. The key factors in getting applause are:

1. Calls for a show of appreciation, 'let's show our appreciation . . .'
2. Comparisons of 'us' and 'them': 'they say that it cannot be done. We say that it can . . .'
3. Introductions. Identify a person – say something about them – pause – name them.
4. Lists of three.
5. Contrasting pairs, elegantly worded antithesis.

It is these last two factors which are unbelievably powerful, particularly when used in conjunction with each other. Typically the message will be complete after the first item on the list, but a rising inflection in the voice signals a continuation to the second item, while a falling inflection on the third item signals the end. There is something inherently satisfying about these sets of three: 'We are united in purpose, strategy, and resolve', *in nomine Patris et Filii et Spiritus Sancti.*

They turn up in children's stories – the three bears, the three billy goats Gruff, the three little pigs. Somehow four little pigs does not sound right.

The other factor mentioned above is that of contrasts: 'Man is born free and everywhere is in chains' (Rousseau); 'That's one small step for man; one giant leap for mankind' (Neil Armstrong). The combination of the two techniques produces a resounding effect; 'Friends, Romans, countrymen, lend me your ears. I come to bury Caesar, not to praise him. The evil that men do lives after them, the good is oft interred with their bones' (Shakespeare, *Julius Caesar*). Once the reader is aware of this structure it will become strikingly noticeable in many contexts. Let us just look at some more examples.

> Government of the people
>   by the people
>   for the people. (Lincoln, Gettysburg)

> Never in the field of human conflict has
> so much been owed by
> so many to
> so few.   (Churchill, 1940)

> Many are called,
> but few are chosen.   (Matthew 22.14)

> This is not the end.
> It is not even the beginning of the end.
> But it is perhaps the end of the beginning.
>   (Churchill, 1942)

It is in the nature of some errors of judgment and human fallibility, such as false assumptions or illogical deduction, that those who fall into the error do not realize their mistake. Similarly there are times when a person uses a particular form of words, or displays some non-verbal behaviour which upsets other people without the originator being aware of it. Although the great virtue of oral communication should be the immediate feedback from the listener, this is not always the case in practice for social and other reasons. The role of the teacher in reflecting the behaviour of the student is therefore of the utmost importance. The art of presenting one's case is essentially a practical one; it is therefore of great value to have an observant and sympathetic listener who can analyse the faults and correct them without destroying the student's confidence. The professional teacher will be well aware of the need for tact and discretion.

The key points that have been covered in this chapter may be listed in the form of a checklist for the potential presenter:

1. Make sure that presentation relates to the listeners. This implies both being aware of their characteristics and also gathering information on their interests and problems.
2. Keep the presentation short.
3. Establish credibility.
4. Never talk down to the audience.
5. Keep the presentation varied and use language, voice, tone, and figures of speech to make it interesting.
6. Make use of pauses.
7. If addressing an audience, rather than participating in an informal discussion there are a number of techniques to obtain applause. Even in the informal surroundings of a small group they may help to emphasize the point. Use contrast and groups of three to produce elegant phrases.
8. Be prepared to listen and adapt.
9. Allow interest and enthusiasm to show!

If at the end of the day your students have acquired the self confidence to speak for themselves, have learnt to express themselves eloquently, imaginatively and with elegance, and can convey passion, fervour and conviction in a dignified and graceful way, then they will be ready to participate fully as citizens and colleagues at work. They may perhaps realize the truth of the old Yiddish proverb, 'All the world is on the tip of the tongue', or failing that perhaps they may reflect on the words of Dionysius the Elder, 'Let thy speech be better than silence, or be silent!'

References and further reading

Adler, Mortimer J (1983) *How to Speak, How to Listen.* Macmillan
Berne, Eric (1975) *What do you Say after you Say Hello?* Corgi
Bligh, Donald (Ed) (1986) *Teach Thinking by Discussion.* SRHE & NFER-Nelson
Bridges, David (1979) *Education, Democracy and Discussion.* NFER
Brown, George and Atkins, Madeleine (1988) *Effective Teaching in Higher Education.* Methuen
Farb, Peter (1974) *Word Play: What Happens when People Talk.* Jonathan Cape
Harnack, R Victor, Thorrel, B Fest and Schindler Jones, Barbara (1977) *Group Discussion: Theory and Technique.* Prentice-Hall
Hill, William Fawcett (1969) *Learning thru Discussion.* Sage
Jaques, David (1984) *Learning in Groups.* Croom Helm
Janis, Irving L (1982) *Groupthink.* Houghton Mifflin
Kolb, David A (1984) *Experiential Learning.* Prentice-Hall
Morris, Jud (1968) *The Art of Listening.* The Industrial Education Institute
Org, Walter J (1982) *Orality and Literacy, the Technology of the Word.* Methuen (New Accents)
Ruby, L (1969) *The Art of Making Sense.* Angus and Robertson
Simons, Herbert W (1986) *Persuasion: Understanding, Practice and Analysis.* Random House
Steil, Layman K et al (1983) *Listening, it can Change your Life.* Wiley
Wardhaugh, Ronald (1985) *How Conversation Works.* Blackwell in association with Deutsch

Index

action plan 68
ad hominem 117
advertisements 123
agora 121
allegory 129
alliteration 130
allusion 130
analogy 109
analysis 107
anaphora 130
antithesis 130
anxiety *see* inhibition
apologies 134
apophasis 130
apostrophe 130
applause 124, 136
argument 108
argumentative discussion 28, 99
Aristotle 32
Armstrong, Neil 137
audience 126
authority 108

Bay of Pigs 95
Berne, Eric 72
Bible 128, 137
Bligh, Donald 29, 42
Bridges, David 54
buzz groups 29, 37, 54

case study 59

cathartic 20, 29
cause and effect 67, 114
chautauqua 121
change 65
Chesterton, G K 92
Churchill, Winston 22, 137
claptrap 136
classical conditioning *see*
        conditioning
closed mind 92
closed question 77
communication 21
comparison 136
conclusion 43
conditioning 124
contrasts 136
cognitive dissonance 125
committee 17, 27, 35, 51
computer 13, 15, 48
consensus 99
conversation 86
courtroom 99
correlation 114
criteria 99
cross-over 30
Cuban Missile Crisis 95
curriculum 47

debating 99
debriefing 26, 59
decision making 94

deduction 103
delivery 128
democracy 22
Descartes 103
description 107
development 123
dialectic 101
dialogue 76, 99
differentiation 109
Dionysius 139
discussion
    argumentative 28
    reflective 28
    functions of 49
    starting 37
disposition 122
disputation 19
distortion 116
diversion 117

Education Reform Act 15
elocution 122
embedded assumptions 117
emotion 62, 89
enthymeme 119
environment 92
equivocation 115
evaluation 42, 88, 95
evidence 26, 101
examples 107
excluded middle 113
experience 59
extending propositions 116

facilitator 12
fact 119
fallacies 113
false analogy 116
family 14, 17
Farb, Peter 21

fear 124
feedback 42, 60, 67
forum 121
frame of reference *see* structures
Froebel, F 18

generalisations 115
glossolalia 126
group 16, 42, 47
    composition 33
    size 34
Group Cognitive Map 39
'Groupthink' 53, 93
group dynamics 42

Harnack, Victor 29
Heller, Joseph 109
hidden agenda 60
Hill, William Fawcett 39
hostage debriefing 63
humility 92
Hymes, Dell 21

incremental change 114
induction 103
inference 91, 119
informative 20
inhibition 52
irony 130
interpretation 87
intervention 55
interview 81
introduction 123
invention 122

Janis, Irving, 93
Jaques, David 29, 42
Julius Caesar 137
judgement 90

Kolb, David 59

languages 19
layout *see* room layout
leader, role of 43
leaderless groups 46
leading question 81
lectures 19, 85
Lincoln, Abraham 22, 137
listen 84
lists 136
literature 19
logic 18, 28, 39, 64, 103, 113

Marshall Plan 95
mean (statistical) 113
meaning 105
memory 12, 122
metaphor 129
moral values 26, 51
Morgan, T 40
motivation 124

National Curriculum 10
negotiation 14, 23
nerves 134
Nixon, President 133
non-conformer 53
non-sequitur 117
non-verbal communication 55,
    135
notes 42, 85, 88, 133

O'Henry 20
open question 77
operant conditioning *see*
    conditioning
oratory 121
oral culture 128
oracy 13

Org, Walter 13

pairs 136
pattern 128
pause 131
Pearl Harbor 95
perception 17
Pericles 16
persuasive 20
phatic 20
phonemes 21
Plato 17, 76, 129
point of view 20, 25
prejudice 100
premisses 100
preparation 23
printing 13, 17
probing 80
projects 11
pronunciation 122
purpose 37, 61
Putnam, David 97

questions 76

Rackham, N 40
radio 13
reasons 132
reductio ad absurdum 112
reflection 59
reflective discussion 28, 99
repetition 11, 19
re-phrasing 56
responding 88
rhetoric 18, 121
rhetorical question 77
Rogers, Carl 89
role-play 11, 14, 59, 71
room layout 35
rote 11

Rousseau, Jean Jacques 137
Runyon, Damon 129

selected instances 115
sensing 87
sequence 79
Shakespeare, W 137
signals 135
silence 82
simile 129
simplification 117
simulation 11, 14, 59
Socrates 76
Socratic method 98
Speakers' Corner 121
speech (oration) 19
standards 99
statistics 14
stereotyping 115
structures 11, 28, 32, 39, 65, 77,
    88, 121
syllogism 104
symbols 106
symmetrical relations 105
syntax 131

Talmud 108
tautology 115

text *see* notes
telephone 14, 20
television 15
temporal sequence 42
Thatcher, Margaret 135
thinking 16, 97
time-out 55
training 15
transactional analysis 72
transitive relations 105
trios 136
Tuckman, B W 42
types of discussion 29, 48

understanding 87
undistributed middle 113
university 19

voice 134
Voltaire 92
Vietnam 95
visits 11

Wardhaugh, Ronald 41
whistle stop 121
work 15, 61, 74
written word 13, 19